There Is Hope

ONE MAN'S JOURNEY
FROM ABUSIVE ANGER
TO
REDEMPTIVE GRACE

James Maxwell

Charlie68 Munster, Indiana

All Scripture quotations are taken from the Authorized King James Bible

Publisher's Note: Many teachers, pastors, authors, and friends are mentioned and quoted herein. The thoughts and opinions herein are the author's alone. Neither the author nor Charlie68 represent any author, pastor, church, organization, or person other than the author himself.

Editors: Rena Fish, Linda Flesher
Proof Reader: Kim Marsack
Cover Layout: Jonathan Lewis, Jonlin Creative, Pekin, Illinois, jonlincreative.com
Cover Photo: James Maxwell
Book Layout © 2016 BookDesignTemplates.com
There is Hope/ James Maxwell. -- 1st edition
ISBN 78-1-7327183-0-20

Dedication

At one point in my recovery, a good friend complimented me on how well he thought I was doing. He asked me what one piece of advice he could give someone else in a similar situation. I replied, "Give him friends like Bob and Darlene Weer, but there are no friends like Bob and Darlene."

The person asking the question was my pastor, John Wilkerson. The truth is that my three-fold cord could not be broken. John, Bob, and Darlene were woven together by the hand of a loving God to fish an unstable, hopeless, and wicked soul from the slimy swamp of pride.

Though her name does not appear in the story to follow, I also owe a debt to a godly woman I knew only at a distance. As I joined the indescribable battle against chronic pain, I could not help but pray for a portion of Kristal Slager's spirit. While cancer slowly stole her from her beloved Bob, her family and friends, and those of us who admired her, she cheerfully told all comers, "I don't have cancer. God has my cancer; I gave it to Him, so He has cancer." Through her brilliant smile, she also declared, "I thank God for cancer!" She opined that the disease had taught her to live. Nearly every week that I saw her, I hugged Kristal and told her that I wanted a portion of her spirit.

I must thank my church, the First Baptist Church of Hammond, Indiana. When I stood before the church family and confessed to my atrocities, they responded with the grace I would want any wayward soul to find.

In gratitude, I dedicate this text to my loving God and pray that He would favor these, my heroes, for any good this work accomplishes. I am the fruit of their love and arduous labor.

CONTENTS

Coming Home

Wednesday, May 3, 2017, was a gorgeous day in Orlando, where I was attending a work-related conference. Just a few days earlier I had left my wife in Arizona to visit with our daughter after we had attended a delightful grade-school musical that she had directed. My wife then arrived home on the night of May 2, one day ahead of me.

At 5:55 on the morning of May 3, I received a text from my wife, and a few minutes later, we spoke on the phone. I went on to the conference and spent the day learning lessons that I am certain were very important, but my wife went silent. I texted Suzanne frequently that morning, but she did not respond.

I left the conference early for the airport and stopped to shop for my wife. I was excited to get home, and I joyfully bought her a new dress, a new bag, and some chocolates. Along the way, I texted her several times and tried to call her a few times, but I never reached her. I checked her location. She was at home—or at least her phone was.

The Uber driver was a personal friend, and we enjoyed our conversation on the way home. Daryl is quite a character, and he has lived in and around the real political scene in Chicago for decades.

I arrived at home shortly after 11:00 p.m. Two friends were waiting in front of my house when I stepped out of the Uber. When they asked if they could come in and speak with me, I couldn't help but notice theirs was not the normal, friendly demeanor I was used to seeing. Both friends had looks on their faces that said, "Little boy, you are going to the principal's office." My heart sank. I dropped the keys, fumbled them into the lock, and then my trembling hand opened the door to an empty house. My friends informed me that they were there for support and that Suzanne had left a note on the table.

I scanned the contents of the note in less than a second, but I was too furious to read it. I crumpled the letter into a tiny ball, slam dunked it into the kitchen garbage, and angrily denounced my wife. "She has NO right to leave me! We had problems, but they were not THAT bad!"

My response was angry and defiant. I tried to be polite and kind, but I was already in the early stages of despair. My friends stayed for a few minutes, listening to my ranting and raving. They left, and I was alone.

The note was not the only object on the table. Her cell phone was also there. We had always shared locations between our phones; I had known where she was, and she had known where I was…that was over. I realized that she had abandoned her phone number. I saw my unread texts, as well as unread texts from others. I saw missed calls and unopened voice messages. She had gone into hiding, and even friends and family would not know where she was.

As I looked at her phone, I remembered making a big deal about taking her to the Verizon store to buy her that iPhone 7 when it was state-of-the-art. I had wanted her to have the best phone in the family. It was expensive, it was nice, and she loved it. She had used it constantly, but now she had left it behind.

Her closet was empty. Her personal items were gone from the bathroom. All of the materials for her tutoring business were gone. The dog cage was gone. Room by room, item by item, inch by inch, and memory by memory, the loneliness crept over my soul. My wife did NOT want to be found; she had taken the dog; the kids were grown, and I had built a decades-old wall of pride between God and myself. I was completely alone.

The night progressed poorly. For a while I was angry and went about to protect myself by checking all of our financial accounts. I found that Suzanne had taken $40 from our joint account and $740 from the account she used for groceries and personal spending. I scoured every financial account, looking for clues as to where she was or what she was doing.

Her car keys were hanging on the refrigerator, and the car was in the driveway. The only key she had kept was the house key. I did think it was nice that she had left me the set of keys with the "clicker," as we had only one remote-entry key. However, I did not know what to think about her keeping a house key. My mind went to evil places, and I imagined she might come back while I was at work in Chicago.

As soon as the hardware store opened on Thursday, I bought new locks and changed all of the locks in the house. Perhaps it was insanity; I was locking out a woman who had no desire to come in. Reality came slowly. I collected all of the credit cards, logged into their online accounts, and changed the passwords. I changed the passwords to the bank accounts. Reality continued to set in slowly.

After more than 24 sleepless hours, and in the midst of selfish despair, I noticed that one of the bank accounts used Suzanne's email address. Through attempting to access that account, I discovered that Suzanne had deleted her email account while in Arizona and had started another. The reality that she would be gone for a long time washed over me again in waves of darkness. Would it be forever? That was not what her note said, but she was so completely gone.

I reactivated the account, looking for additional financial clues. Suzanne had deleted all of her recent messages and had removed them from the trash. She had a rule set to forward her email to a new account.

Panic.

For thirty years I had thought that I was in control. *Control*: that was a word which would soon begin to teach me many lessons. We mortals live borrowed lives on a planet created by the omnipotent, sovereign God of the universe. Every breath is in His hands. Our thoughts are open to Him, He knows our hearts, and it is He who is in control.

What substance is most addictive? Is it heroine? Cocaine? Nicotine? The illusion of control rivals all of them. Like any junkie, I was searching everywhere for an ounce of my power. My mind bent itself in every direction, wildly seeking to find control, power, authority, or any vestige of the emotional fiefdom of my fantasies. The reality of what I had been became a bear trap snapped closed on my soul, and like a wild animal, I would have chewed off my soul to break free, but alas, my soul is beyond my reach. Souls, too, are in God's domain.

Isaiah 14:12-17

How art thou fallen from heaven, O Lucifer, son of the morning! How art thou cut down to the ground, which didst weaken the nations! For thou hast said in thine heart, I will ascend into heaven, I will exalt my throne above the stars of God: I will sit also upon the mount of the congregation, in the sides of the north. I will ascend above the heights of the clouds; I will be like the most High. Yet thou shalt be brought down to hell, to the sides of the pit.

As Satan in the ages past imagined himself to be like the most High, I had imagined myself to be the lord of my home. Allegiance to me, which had been the paramount rule, had now been broken. In the mystical kingdom of my mind, no one was to question me, and no one was to speak of "private family matters" outside of my castle. Out there—somewhere out in the world beyond my control—my most loyal subject was in open rebellion. She was telling my secrets and defying my will.

Like Saul of Tarsus, I had used a rod of iron to wreak great havoc while convincing my subjects (or so I thought) and myself that I was the friend of God in this matter.

Cognitive dissonance is the term describing the mental stress created by believing what we know to be false. I knew that my rage and anger were ungodly, but I also "knew" that my wife was to be in complete submission to me. I knew that I was responsible to bring up my children in the nurture and admonition of the LORD, but I also "knew" that as the lord of my house, they were to do my every bidding. They were expected to believe my every word as truth. Truth: the "truths" of my mind were being crushed to death by the unflinching truth of reality.

I had put myself at the top of the pyramid of our home. In my mind, I was the gateway to God. I interpreted what He said, what He meant, and what He wanted. Cognitive dissonance: I knew that every one of us must give an account of himself to God, but I thought I knew that I was His deputy in our home. I knew that my wrath and dictatorial control were wrong and that He demands clean vessels, but I thought I knew that my wife and children were to side with me when they believed differently about the nature of God or the commands of God. This death comes at the end of the sin of pride. If one would avoid the crushing harm of sin such as mine, this is where the axe must be laid to the root of the tree.

The next day the battle of "truth" against truth raged on. I fired off an email in the middle of the night to Suzanne's new account. I was hardly coherent.

I opened our safe to see if the credit cards were still in there. My .45 was gone. I looked behind the bed; my shotgun was also gone. I felt partially betrayed and partially thankful that Suzanne had apparently tried to prevent a suicide attempt. She knew me well. I went to the living room. The shotgun above the television was still in its usual place. I went to my office; the .22 was still there. Suzanne had recently gone with me to purchase 500 rounds of ammunition for it. I laughed out loud, finding dark humor in the fact that the hidden guns were gone, but that the obvious guns were still in our house.

Somewhere in the night, I found that I was blocked from Facebook. As I wandered mindlessly through the house, I found more and more items missing. Her favorite photos were gone. My wife had not slipped away for a short time; she had moved out. The raging river of reality continued to sweep me from my feet and plunge me into the icy rapids of emotional distress.

I had received my "Dear John" letter. Had I truly read it, I could have found sanity in real truth, but my imagination would not yet allow me to face the real truth. Nevertheless, understanding what she had said was important. I went to the trash can, dug out the letter, carefully smoothed out the wrinkled paper I had so angrily wadded into a ball, and read the following words:

Dear Sweetheart,

I LOVE YOU

Without a shadow of a doubt, I love you and am glad to be your wife. I want to be your wife. I love being your wife. I made a decision last night that was probably the most difficult decision that I have ever made. I made a decision to go to a safe place until both of us have sought help—you with your anger issues and me with my fear. I took Mocha (the dog) with me.

For almost 30 years we have struggled with anger issues. When you [committed the final actions that convinced her she needed to make a change], you crossed a line. You need help, and so do I. I am willing to get help and will be seeking help. It is my longing and desire that you seek professional and spiritual help for your medical and spiritual issues. Until you can prove to me by having those counselors call me and let me know that it is safe to return, I am gone to a safe place.

Only a very few people know where my safe place is. [Our son, daughter-in-law, and daughter] all support me, and they also support you. They want us both to get the help we need. The decision to separate for a while is MY decision, and I did not go to [my son's house] or to [my daughter's house] because I did not want to drag the kids into this. They did not make this decision, and they love and want the best for both of us.

I LOVE you, and sometimes love does the hard thing. It is obvious to me after 30 years of struggling with some of the same issues, our methods aren't working. You need space and time alone and with counsel to dig out the deep issues that cause you to react with anger toward me. Your reaction to the article that I wrote a few weeks ago was only a symptom of a bigger problem that has been plaguing us for so long. That four days of struggling with you really drained me physically, and I am positive it was draining on you as well.

Please, please get help. When it is appropriate, I will be willing to set up a time and place with boundaries to talk to you on the phone to discuss our issues and how we are dealing with them. I WANT to talk to you. I LOVE you!! I just know from past experience that talking to you on the phone right now would not help our situation.

I love YOU!

Your Angel

Jeremiah 29:11, *For I know the thoughts that I think toward you, saith the LORD, thoughts of peace, and not of evil, to give you an expected end.*

PS: With all of my heart, I want YOU and a healthy happy US. My heart's goal is reconciliation and restoration because I love you.

Suzanne Marie

There was no sleep for me on Wednesday night. On Thursday morning during some rare lucid moments, I took steps to make sure I could go on living. I bought bottled water and dropped my clothes off to be laundered.

I began to crave sleep. Around 1:00 p.m., I was in the bathtub trying to relax for another attempt to sleep when I heard a knock at the door. Wild with fantasies, I partially dried off and went to the door in a bathrobe. Bob and Darlene Weer were waiting for me. Darlene said,"The Holy Spirit told me to come to check on Suzanne because something's wrong. What's wrong with Suzanne?"

In a distraught emotional fit, I invited them in and then rushed to my room to put on clothes. By the time the Weers had arrived, I had already filled the contents of two boxes of Kleenex and a partial role of paper towels with tears and nasal mucus. My continued sobbing, heaving, and wailing were intense. Bob called Pastor John Wilkerson.

The Weers and Pastor Wilkerson together decided that I should not stay in the house alone overnight. Around 4:00 I left with the Weers. The three of them had spent three hours calming me down and helping me prepare to leave the house and go with the Weers. At one point Darlene wrapped her arms around my shoulders and said, "I am NOT leaving. You cannot be alone in this house tonight."

Bob and Darlene made sure I ate. I did not eat much, but they made sure I ate. Late that afternoon I lay down and fell "asleep" for about 90 minutes; mine was a horrid state of unconsciousness. I had constant nightmares that are what I would think a bad LSD trip would be like. No people were in my dream—only walls, shapes, and a world that moved, shook, and displayed itself in vibrant colors. In a sense, I was asleep, but I do not believe my mind rested at all. That night, there was still no sleep. I was unbelievably thirsty all night. While trying to rest "in bed," I consumed an entire gallon of water and made frequent trips to the bathroom.

Seest thou a man wise in his own conceit? There is more hope of a fool than of him. – Proverbs 26:12

Even the fool has hope. He has more hope than I had. Consequences abound, but there is hope. The God of all hope never sleeps. I was there. I was the man with less hope than a fool. I was a man in need of repentance, but my story did not start on May 3, 2017. The path to repentance began in the pit of sin.

HOPEFUL HELPS

- There is always hope.
- Women in abusive relationships need help.
- When we have fallen, we need help.
- Beware of pride.

Author's Notes

Please read what comes hereafter with a generous sprinkling of grace. In the pages to follow I speak plainly to many subjects and dogmatically to many doctrines. In person, I tend to speak in a forthright manner. Please pardon any misguided strokes of my pen.

As to misguided strokes of my pen, please note that this is a narrative. I often quote from the journal I kept during the worst days. Opinions reflected therein are the opinions I had during those dark days. I did not mask them, but they are only indicative of my thoughts and feelings on that particular day.

As to my right to write on any topic in this book, I have none. I am not the shining example of redemption whose faith it is fit to follow; but rather, the redeemed former monster of a true-to-life horror story. I have never published a book before, and much of what I have written crosses boundaries in the arenas of doctrine and of domestic abuse.

When one speaks to the Scripture, he or she must speak prophetically. Matters of doctrine must be presented plainly. It may be that your doctrine, dear friend, differs from mine. I respect that, and I respect your right and responsibility to read with discernment.

I do not pretend to be an expert or an authority. I am simply your humble servant, acknowledging who and what I am, and praying that *the God of all comfort who comforteth us in all our tribulation* may enable me to comfort you *with the same comfort wherewith I myself have been comforted of God.* (**Paraphrased** from 2 Corinthians 1:3, 4).

Looking Back

In October of 1983, I asked Suzanne Dow to be my date at an upcoming fall program banquet for the bus ministry at Hyles-Anderson College. She accepted. It was a beautiful night, but I had no idea before that night who she really was. A mutual friend had basically dared me to ask Suzanne out by promising to pay for my banquet ticket if she declined. Sure that she would turn me down flat, I asked, and surprisingly, she accepted.

The dinner was little more than dining room fare, but the bus ministry program was inspiring. Suzanne and I left the chapel excited about the joy of bringing families to church on our buses, and then we were left to ourselves. There were game rooms and other quiet venues. Somewhere in the crowded halls of that Bible college, an angel from Heaven became a thief; Suzanne stole my heart.

When I returned to my dorm room, I excitedly told my roommates, "I'm going to marry that girl!"

"You're crazy!" they chorused.

We dated for four years, but our "dating" was not the same dating that people mean by the term today. During those four years, we were under the rules of a Bible college that prohibited any touching whatsoever. We did not have unchaperoned dates anywhere, except for a few times when I traveled to Maine to visit her. Our first kiss was at the altar when her father said, "You may kiss the bride."

Suzanne and I had bumps, and I gave her reasons to question whether or not I was the right guy, but during our dating, there were no episodes of anger or control issues. Our engagement was a different story. While there were certainly no displays of violence, there were many incidents of manipulation and increasing efforts at control. Most of my attempts were silly and petty, but had anyone known the truth, I was exerting significant signs of control.

Control equals pride. Pride equals blind sin. There is no end to the damage of a man's usurping God.

My first horrific outburst occurred during our engagement. During a discussion about some topic I cannot remember, I went into a rage publicly. I snatched a soda can from her hand and crushed it while bellowing savagely at the most gentle soul you could ever imagine. My tirade was an awful one-time event. Thirty-two years later I cannot even tell you what silly exchange aroused my rage.

The dean at our college warned us at that time that we could wind up "really good and divorced" if we did not deal with my anger. I should have sought help then. She would have been justified in dropping me like a hot potato without ever looking back, but I wooed her with all the charm I had, and eventually we were married.

Suzanne's parents had concerns, and they voiced them. She was living at home in Maine for the six months prior to our wedding. Our original wedding date was June 13, but she broke our engagement before we had printed invitations. By the time we were reconciled, the earliest available date was July 2.

A week or so before the wedding, Suzanne called me. She was uncertain again and wanted to call off the wedding. This time, I became defiant and shouted, "You can't call off this wedding!"

"What do you mean I can't call off the wedding?" she asked.

"Suzanne, my whole family has non-refundable airline tickets! We can't do this again. They have paid thousands of dollars to be there for our wedding on July 2, and we're getting married on July 2!"

Believe it or not, that excuse about my family "worked." We were married on July 2, 1987, and she was the most gorgeous bride anyone has ever seen. The wedding was long, but beautiful. The reception was happy and nostalgic. We were as poor as a couple of church mice, but nobody cared. That day was truly beautiful...and then it wasn't.

Scarcely 48 hours after we left our wedding reception, I lost my temper for the first time. I went nuts because...because I was lost in traffic in Schenectady, New York. That I was lost in traffic was the fault of those Yankees who had made the poorly written street signs! I used a well-known adjective associated with Yankees in my youth. In fact, I cursed and swore and behaved like an animal—even though nothing is ever accomplished by swearing. When I came to myself, I apologized profusely and then went on to "lose my temper" just about every day for the next several years. The tale of those years would read like a Stephen King novel. Every imaginable horror, and a few that a normal person could never imagine, happened in our "home."

With an apology to veterans, it may be that no war hero has ever conducted himself more valiantly than Suzanne. She was tortured verbally, emotionally, and sometimes physically for years. In the midst of those years, she maintained herself as the kindest, sweetest, most gentle and loving soul one could ever meet.

Of necessity to note is that both of our children were born in those first years, which means that twice she suffered through the unimaginable during her pregnancies and through nursing her babies. She lived through hell with her own private tormentor.

Some attempts were made at intervention. Her mother tried, one of our former pastors tried, and Suzanne herself tried to coax me to seek help. Intervention did not happen at all until April of 1996. Three months short of our eighth anniversary, God began to show me the path to repentance while I was on a business trip in Washington, D.C. My normal habit was to read a novel between work and bedtime. Usually I read a western novel with the same storyline—the good guy always got the girl after some displays of violence. This night I was out of books, so I turned on the television.

I happened upon the John Ritter made-for-television movie titled *Unforgivable: The Paul Hegstrom Story*. This true story details the life of a violently abusive husband who narrowly averted prison time for attempted murder. Paul was reformed and went on to help others with their anger issues. I almost changed the channel because the story was so repugnant, but I recognized myself in the storyline. As I forced myself to watch, and at the very hour, my rage and anger started down the path of reform. I experienced an instant change, but one that was incomplete and sometimes superficial.

Starting in 1996 and continuing through most of 2015, I continually improved in the areas of rage and anger. The mechanism I chose to cope with was silence. When I first felt rage coming on, I would simply stop talking. I would then turn my heart upward and look to heaven for help. This worked. I was not always perfect at it, but keeping silent worked. Day by day and year by year, practicing this procedure made me better at it.

Even during the so-called "good" years, I faced crisis moments. Some of them were every bit as bad as the first years. The time between crisis moments gradually grew from days to weeks to months. When Suzanne left, eight years had passed since I had touched anyone in anger. Prior to December 19, 2015, it had been a very long time since I had gone into a rage.

Although the calm between the storms had grown large at times, there were always cracks in the foundation of my relationship with my wife. The way that Suzanne maintained her sweet, gentle, godly spirit for all of those decades has no human explanation. Those who know her could never imagine what she survived. Suzanne is a miracle.

Our kids can remember the many times of crisis. Those days were like Hell to them, but they never saw the first days and cannot know how dark those days were.

Two thousand fifteen was our best year ever. We had joy and friendship. The rage and anger were so well under control that I even taught others about it. I confessed to people that I had been an angry, abusive person and told them how they could be better like me. I did not know how far I was from "better."

As Saul of Tarsus, I went about causing destruction, as though I were doing God some favor. I was bold and confident in my blasphemy.

My wife and I served in ministries at our church. I was a deacon, we both taught Sunday school; we helped with widows in our church; I helped in small ways with the finances of our church; Suzanne was in the choir and other music ministries; she was a member of the Women's Missionary Society and had served as an officer—what was there to fix? When I finally made my confession before our church, nearly everyone was shocked. Their shock was because we humans observe what we can see, but God looks upon the heart, and my heart was still ruled by pride.

Through 2015 Suzanne and I both knew that we had something special. God had indeed convicted me of the sins of rage and anger, and He was beginning to show me *my* wife belonged to **Him** rather than to me. For nineteen years my vice of control had been gradually diminishing. July of 2008 was the last time I had touched anyone in anger, and on the surface, everything looked as though it was heading in the right direction. We were edging toward full repentance, but we never unearthed the root cause. I had never repented of my pattern of idolatry in attempting to take God's role in the life of His precious daughter.

God truly uses the circumstances of our lives to draw us to Him. For me to see my pride and know that I needed Him, God had to strip me of my ability to stand in my own strength.

Saturday, December 19, 2015, at 8:30 a.m was a definite time and date etched in my memory. I was cooking breakfast for my wife and daughter when the pain started. At first I felt just a pinch in my thigh, but it grew. By the time I put the food on the table, I was visibly grimacing. My daughter asked me if I was all right, and I growled some sort of short answer. Within minutes I was curled up in a fetal position on my bed.

It took Suzanne about 45 minutes to dress me. After that she and our daughter labored to get me into a car. They even considered an ambulance. Eventually we made our way to our immediate care facility. The triage nurse immediately put me in a wheelchair. Shortly thereafter, we met with a doctor. After an exam and an injection, I was sent home with painkillers for what appeared to be sciatica.

A month later the pain was no better. My doctor sent me for imaging. After a few rounds of CAT scans and MRIs, I learned that I had a rare nerve-pain condition. In the next fifteen months, I would see more than ten doctors, four of whom were neurosurgeons. An advocacy group sent my case notes to Mayo Clinic where the doctors understood my condition, but could do nothing to help.

The pain was relentless. We saw doctor after doctor after doctor. Nobody knew what to do with my condition, so the doctors decided to address the issue with a spinal cord stimulator. A stimulator is a battery connected to a set of electrodes that are implanted directly on the spine so that the nerves can receive direct "stimulation" in the form of electrical pulses. The electrical pulses create white noise so that the brain cannot discern pain. For one week I had electrodes in my back with cords running out to an external controller that allowed me to adjust the stimulations in several ways.

Prior to scheduling a permanent implant, my neurosurgeon-de-jour ordered tests that showed the condition had caused permanent nerve damage along a large nerve in one leg. Though the stimulator was marginally helpful, we decided against having a permanent implant for several reasons. The pain persisted.

For fifteen months I was in pain every moment of my life. Some pain was always waxing and waning in a couple of areas, but the truest torment came from the sudden pains. A random spot on my body could be painless one second, but the next second, I would be suffering with intense stabbing or burning or shooting pain. Often these sudden pains would last for only seconds. Sometimes the entire left side of my body would be involved, and the pain would last for hours.

On a few occasions, Suzanne wandered into our bedroom and found me flat on my back with tears running into my ears. Though I did not have any specific plan for suicide, I did not want to live. I did not necessarily want death; I did not want to lose the good qualities of life, but I simply could not bear the idea of continuing to live in that level of pain. I had conjured thoughts of how to die without making the suicide obvious so that Suzanne could collect life insurance benefits.

The pain continues to this day, though an extensive readjustment of my medications shortly after Suzanne left helped immensely. I have hopes of getting some help from John's Hopkins in Baltimore. Doctors there have a curative procedure that is more than 76 percent successful.

Yes, I have had physical pain, but neither pain nor any other trial causes one to hurt people. Pain does not cause sin. The drugs did not cause my crimes. Circumstances can never be used as scapegoats.

What the drugs did do was to make me more prone to mood swings and fallacious thinking. Coupled with the pain, the drugs helped strip the veneer of mind games that covered the rotting decay of my soul. The rage and anger returned with a vengeance—an important turning point in my life. The strength of my will was gone, and my core was all that was left. This condition revealed the fact that my coping mechanisms were not spiritual answers to spiritual problems. They were carnal procedures that evaporated when my emotional strength had been depleted.

God chastises, and when one does not yield, when one does not submit to His transforming grace, He knows how to help. Correction is meant to yield the peaceable fruit of righteousness. God has predestinated His own to be conformed to the image of his Son, and His predestination is immutable.

In the weeks and months leading up to April 14, we had discussed the issues of control and her individual personhood. We had been making progress in understanding what marriage should be. Little by little and bit by bit, Suzanne was growing to understand her own personhood. She was and is an individual who stands before God by herself in her own right and as a beloved daughter of the Most High.

These steps were small and slow. Moreover, they did not address the core problem I had. While there are Biblical roles in marriage, the role of Christ as the loving Saviour of the body was a role I had never played. The Christ who washed the feet of the disciples, teaching that the greatest must be the servant was a role I had never played. Instead, I played the part of the Greek god, Zeus. In doing so, I arrogantly misrepresented the image of Christ.

Any authority of man is limited, and a husband serves at God's pleasure under the ultimate headship of Christ. Usurping His place is the highest form of pride, and this is blasphemy.

Hebrews 12:5-8

And ye have forgotten the exhortation which speaketh unto you as unto children, My son, despise not thou the chastening of the LORD, nor faint when thou art rebuked of him: for whom the LORD loveth he chasteneth, and scourgeth every son whom he receiveth. If ye endure chastening, God dealeth with you as with sons; for what son is he whom the father chasteneth not? But if ye be without chastisement, whereof all are partakers, then are ye bastards, and not sons.

On April 14, 2017, I threw an outrageous fit after reading a letter my wife had written to our son. In the letter she had listed all of the important, positive influences in her life. My name was not on the list. Common sense would tell anyone why I was not on the list, but not seeing my name was quite a blow to my ego. I was far too self-centered to let the matter pass.

I knew that my reaction was unreasonable and out of line with reality. I knew my emotions were overblown. I knew I was about to lose my temper and could feel the rancor inside. I made an awful choice, and I opened my mouth. I screamed, stomped, slammed, and berated for hours. Suzanne began to bolt, and I threatened to kill myself. I was (pardon the pun) dead serious. I was losing control, and I knew it. That night I crossed some important spiritual lines.

Anyone who would have seen me that night would have done anything in his or her power to rescue Suzanne. I was serious because that night I knew I had lost control. The silence coping mechanism was over, and I knew Suzanne had seen enough. For the next four days, I replayed the events of April 14, trying to convince her that what happened was her fault. Dodging responsibility had not been a crime of mine before, but now I was desperate. While my wife remained very kind and ever-loving, part of me knew that I was skating on very thin ice.

On April 27, Suzanne and I flew to Phoenix to watch our daughter direct a grade-school musical. On our way there, I was very concerned that our daughter, who is a strong woman in own her rights, would try to convince Suzanne to leave me. I told Suzanne not to mention our problems to our daughter, but rather to wait to address them when we got home. "Suzanne, if she asks how we are doing, tell her that we are fine," I ordered.

The next evening I could feel myself becoming agitated again. I confessed it to Suzanne, and she helped calm me. Because I had become agitated yet again, the next day would be my last chance. Suzanne asked me once more to seek help with a particular counselor. I told her that there was no use because my problems were out of his league. I did not know what to do. In a few hours I would leave, knowing I had failed.

The next morning I hugged and kissed my wife with the false hope that I would do so again in just a few days. I got in the car and left for a business trip in Florida while Suzanne stayed for a few more days with our daughter. She flew home on May 2, arriving around 11:00 p.m.

On Wednesday, May 3, I had a phone call with Suzanne. Later that morning—around 10:00 a.m.—she went silent and did not respond to my texts or calls.

HOPEFUL HELPS

- Do not wait for calamity; if you need help, seek it decisively!
- Thank God for His mercy in whatever trials He uses to bring you to Himself.
- Neither pain nor our personal trials are excuses to hurt others.
- Beware of the human heart; not only is it capable of deception, but without Christ it is desperately wicked. (Jeremiah 17:9)
- As I said before and will say again, beware of pride.

Waking Up

I took an Uber home from the airport, and as we approached the house, I saw a van parked in front. Our car was still in the driveway. As I stepped out of the car, two friends emerged from the van. I saw their stern looks and immediately knew why Suzanne hadn't answered my calls or texts. *She's gone!* my mind screamed.

On July 2, 1987, I married the godliest, sweetest, most amazing woman ever. On April 14, 2017, I lost her. Rather, in 29 years, 9 months, and 12 days, I had driven her away.

Jesus explained a bit about Hell in the account of a beggar named Lazarus and a rich man.

There was a certain rich man, which was clothed in purple and fine linen, and fared sumptuously every day: and there was a certain beggar named Lazarus, which was laid at his gate, full of sores, and desiring to be fed with the crumbs which fell from the rich man's table: moreover the dogs came and licked his sores. And it came to pass, that the beggar died, and was carried by the angels into Abraham's bosom: the rich man also died, and was buried; and in hell he lift up his eyes, being in torments, and seeth Abraham afar off, and Lazarus in his bosom. And he cried and said, Father Abraham, have mercy on me, and send Lazarus, that he may dip the tip of his finger in water, and cool my tongue; for I am tormented in this flame. But Abraham said, Son, remember that thou in thy lifetime receivedst thy good things, and likewise Lazarus evil things: but now he is comforted, and thou art tormented. And beside all this, between us and you there is a great gulf fixed: so that they which would pass from hence to you cannot; neither can they pass to us, that would come from thence. Then he said, I pray thee therefore, father, that thou wouldest send him to my father's house: for I have five brethren; that he may testify unto them, lest they also come into this place of torment (Luke 16:19-31).

Please bear with me and for a moment, allow me to speak with the voice of that rich man in Hell. If you are a man with the sins of pride or rage or anger, then you are my "brother." Please, please, please! Do not enter my place of torment! By any means necessary, turn to the God of Heaven for mercy before you commit my sins. Please allow me to testify to you lest you hurt those you love as I have hurt those whom I love with all of my heart. Please, please, please repent.

The venom of pride will silently poison your soul. If you are given to anger, you are filled with pride. The blindness of pride keeps you chained to the cell of your insanity. Those who have never seen you with your control mechanisms in action may think you to be humble, but you know the truth (and those who live with you know the truth). You know that the license for your actions comes from placing yourself above others. You know that to *Let nothing be done through strife or vainglory; but in lowliness of mind...esteem other[s] better than yourself* is beyond you.

Pride, to paraphrase the wisdom of one of my teachers, is "self-sufficiency, self-importance, self-serving, and self-centered. Pride is all about what I want. Humility is dying to self as God commanded in Romans 6:11. (*Likewise reckon ye also yourselves to be dead indeed unto sin, but alive unto God through Jesus Christ our Lord.*)

Repentance is a gift from God that you desperately need. God must bring repentance to the human heart, and when He does, it can grow. It can grow IF it is met with a full surrender to Christ. Surrender is not a one-time deed, but rather it is a path. It is a vital part of daily prayer.

Matthew 4:17 describes the beginning of Jesus' ministry this way: *From that time Jesus began to preach, and to say, Repent: for the kingdom of heaven is at hand.*

While God's servants provide instruction, God Himself gives repentance, and so it was with me. On the morning of May 5, after more than fifty hours with only snippets of troubled sleep, God brought me to sincere repentance. I was not seeking repentance; I was not aware that I needed to repent. I knew that I had done some wrong, but I was also convinced that my wife was completely out of line for leaving me. I was standing in Bob Weer's kitchen around 6:00 a.m. when he walked in and graciously asked if I might like some eggs for breakfast. I could not answer him; I doubled over as though someone had punched me in the gut, and I fell sobbing to the floor. My heart cried out to God.

As I sobbed and heaved uncontrollably, I begged the LORD to forgive me and change me. These tears were different from the ones I had shed on Thursday, the day I came home to the empty house. On that day, it was about me and what I had lost. Now it was about me and whom I had hurt; about me and what I had done; about me and who I had been. Those tears were about me being restored to my God.

This repentance was the turning point on my road to restoration. This was the pivotal moment of my adult life. Much, much, much has happened since, and I have seen the hand of God in my life. I can irrevocably say that Friday morning on the floor of Bob Weer's kitchen, the LORD changed my life.

From that point on, my constant prayer became:

"LORD, please heal Suzanne."

"LORD, please change me."

"Father, please restore us."

Whenever anyone told me that they were praying for me, I replied, "Pray that God heals Suzanne, changes me, and restores our marriage." The last point quickly changed, I did not want THAT marriage to be restored. The last point became a request for a brand-new marriage; I wanted God to create something that had never existed before.

In Matthew 6:6, Jesus said,

But thou, when thou prayest, enter into thy closet, and when thou hast shut thy door, pray to thy Father which is in secret; and thy Father which seeth in secret shall reward thee openly.

I cannot put a name to the prayers, but I am convinced that someone was praying for me on the morning of May 6, 2017. God very clearly gave me a gift for which I had never asked. Truly, *the effectual fervent prayer of a righteous man availeth much.*

Bob and Darlene gave themselves entirely to me on Friday. They took me home to pick up the house and set it in order so that I could live there. We bought a small sack of groceries and took care of necessary chores.

Mostly the day was given to seeking God. God bless Bob and Darlene who stayed with the business of arranging the house. Again and again, I went into the spare bedroom to cry out and make my confession. I emptied more boxes of tissues with my tears, but no sleep came.

Sometimes small steps lead down good paths. While we were at the house on Friday, as I had my phone connected to a charger in the kitchen, my playlist from Spotify with roughly a hundred godly, uplifting songs played non-stop. Before we left the house that day, Darlene admonished me, "Jim, you keep that good, godly music playing." She was emphatic, and she was right.

In I Samuel 16 God tells the story of how Saul was refreshed from the evil spirit that troubled him when David played godly music (as is assumed because David was the musician and psalmist) upon his harp. Music is powerful, and a man in my state needed right music. I was entering the world of isolation, and that playlist would prove to be one of my very best friends. For months I played it constantly. If I was alone at home, driving, working at the office, or anywhere I could play my godly, uplifting music, I did play it.

I cannot clap in rhythm; I do not frequently sing on tune. I am anything but a musician, and yet I can strongly recommend godly, spiritual music for a tormented soul. The torments I faced were those of my own making, but skillful musicians had provided a useful crutch; it helped me.

Meanwhile, back at the ranch, the Devil was setting traps and preparing an ambush. Seriously, in the midst of a crisis, there are many moving parts, and many of them have the potential for harm. Satan, as a roaring lion, is still going about seeking whom he may devour, and wounded animals are easy prey for lions. Several miscues on my part in the early hours caused further hurt.

I began calling close family members. With no way to know what Suzanne was thinking, I told the story from the perspective of a bewildered soul searching for the truth. I told them what was missing from the house, what clues I had found in bank accounts, and who knows what else. What I did not know was that some of my family already knew what had happened, and they were not happy. Some of what I said made its way back to Suzanne from a very different perspective than mine. My clues about the money she had moved sounded to some as though I was accusing her of stealing. Certainly people repeat what they hear from their own perspectives, and *In the multitude of words there wanteth not sin, but he that refraineth his lips is wise* (Proverbs 10:19).

At some point on Friday, I realized that I held positions of leadership in our church. I was a deacon, a Sunday school teacher, and a leader in the Reformers Unanimous addiction program. I had positions of leadership, but I was no leader. That I should pretend to lead others when I was such a personal train wreck was neither fit nor fitting. I called the church and resigned every office and duty.

Around 1:00 I re-read Suzanne's "Dear-John" letter. She wanted me to get professional help. I texted Pastor Wilkerson for advice, and he responded almost immediately with a contact for Refuge Christian Counseling in South Holland. The moment his text hit my phone, I called them and left a message asking for an appointment.

For nearly thirty years, Suzanne and I had known that I needed help of some kind. We never knew where to turn. Somehow I had the answer within two minutes when I really wanted it. Proverbs 18 begins with these words, *Through desire a man, having separated himself, seeketh and intermeddleth with all wisdom.*

Separate myself I did. From that point on, I had only two purposes in life: to become the man God wanted me to be and to prepare for my wife's return. Every single thing I did from May 5 on was focused on those two goals. If I went to work, I worked to provide for the two of us. If I ate, I ate for fuel to serve God and prepare for Suzanne.

My own desires and even pleasures had ruled much of our lives. I needed a pure soul with which to seek God. I changed my diet almost exclusively to beans and quinoa. I did not butter or season them. I wanted my food to be for fuel—not as a source of pleasure or comfort. I needed a soul that could seek God. I needed freedom from the habits of serving myself.

God instructs His children in James 4:8-10 "*Draw nigh to God, and he will draw nigh to you. Cleanse your hands, ye sinners; and purify your hearts, ye double minded. Be afflicted, and mourn, and weep: let your laughter be turned to mourning, and your joy to heaviness. Humble yourselves in the sight of the Lord, and he shall lift you up.*" My way of afflicting myself is not the point, nor am I any expert on seeking humility. I was stumbling in the dark, but any Christian who would seek Christ help from pit of pride would do well to meditate on these verses and to ask the Holy Ghost for guidance in the right way to do so.

Paul told the church at Galatia that ...*if a man be overtaken in a fault, ye which are spiritual, restore such an one in the spirit of meekness; considering thyself, lest thou also be tempted.* (Galatians 6:1) He instructed Timothy that *"the servant of the LORD must not strive; but be gentle unto all men, apt to teach, patient, in meekness instructing those that oppose themselves; if God peradventure will give them repentance to the acknowledging of the truth; and that they may recover themselves out of the snare of the devil, who are taken captive by him at his will."* (II Timothy 2:24-26)

The journey of restoration is not for the faint of heart and is not to be attempted alone. Pastor Wilkerson took the apostle (and the LORD) at his word and checked in frequently. For the first many days, the pastor made contact with me multiple times a day. As an under-shepherd working in

Christ's stead, he ran to my side. *Brethren, if any of you do err from the truth, and one convert him; let him know, that he which converteth the sinner from the error of his way shall save a soul from death, and shall hide a multitude of sins.* (James 5:19-20) Make no mistake, without the ministries of Pastor Wilkerson, Bob Weer, Deacon Jon, Wayne (a successful businessman who has been my friend for decades), and many others, my story would have no happy ending. I had created a horrific train wreck of godlessness, and my recovery required an army.

At the time of this writing, I have recently come from a meeting where I heard a pastor from another state mention the subject of spousal abuse. He claimed to have told his church that if he knew of such a man in his congregation, he and the men of the church would "baptize him with baseball bats," and he continued, "And I mean it." Perhaps he did. Perhaps such a baptism would be just punishment, but it is one that should never happen.

Should such a "baptism" ever be administered, the pastor and his men would subject themselves to the jail sentence deserved by the abuser; that miscarriage of justice alone makes his statement a bad idea. More to the point, Pastor Wilkerson better served the world by helping remove an abusive man from the social ecosystem. Threats only worsen the problem. The pastor with the baseball bats has insured that no abusive man in his congregation will ever approach him for help, but worse than that, he has warned abusers to move their victims to other places and to otherwise insulate themselves from his influence. He has pushed the problem further underground.

God provided governments to deal with crimes and to provide protection from violence. Governmental intervention is necessary and proper in many, if not most cases. As citizens, it may be incumbent upon pastors or other church members to contact or cooperate with law enforcement. Even that responsibility is hindered by public threats and chest thumping; abusive men will simply take their victims elsewhere.

Churches are instructed on how to handle offenses in Matthew 18 and I Corinthians 6. The goal of the LORD's servant should be to meekly instruct offenders so that they may recover themselves from Satan's snares. Churches are important places with an abundance of power and opportunity to instruct and inform. By the grace of God, it was my blessing to belong to a church that serves God in such a way.

I retired early on Friday night. In the guest room at the Weer's house, I lay in bed searching the web on my phone. I was trying to learn all that I could about recovering from spousal abuse. One fact became clear early on—reconciliation was rare. I could not find (and have still not found) any substantive advice for reconciling a marriage after there has been physical abuse. I searched any and every way I could think of, but what I was looking for did not seem to exist.

Somewhere in the darkness, I found a YouTube video entitled *Shepherding the Emotionally Destructive Marriage,* featuring a lady named Leslie Vernick and a gentleman named Chris Moles. These Christian people were working together on my problem, and they had my attention. I watched the video and immediately ordered the books *The Emotionally Destructive Marriage* by Leslie Vernick and *The Heart of Domestic Abuse* by Chris Moles. I even checked the option to pay more for next day delivery.

In the next four months I would read thousands of pages, and many of the books would help change my life, but outside of the Bible itself, few other titles would have quite the impact of these two books. Later, I would find a book I like even more, but Chris Moles and Leslie Vernick set the tone for my recovery. I cannot thank God enough for leading me to that video.

Suzanne and I were completely separated one from the other, but within forty-eight hours of each other, we both watched *Shepherding the Emotionally Destructive Marriage.* The video had a profound, but different, impact on each of us. For me, I began to understand the nature, depth, and consequences of my sin. It was painful—very painful—but it was pivotal. In the same video, my now estranged wife found hope. Hope is a powerful panacea.

Books became an important piece to my puzzle. On Amazon alone I would order nineteen different books in the first four months of my restoration. I would read a few others at home, and friends would lend me yet others. *Through desire a man, having separated himself, seeketh and intermeddleth with all wisdom.* (Proverbs 18:1) I was "all-in," and books were some of my key resources.

Repentance is a gift of God. I had not known that I needed it. I was not seeking it, but God gave it to me. Right there on the floor of Bob Weer's kitchen, a miracle began. My counselors had been gentle and patient. Nobody prodded me into repentance. Nobody had chastised me at all.

Three spiritual first responders had come to my aid in compassion. They had administered the Biblical first aid of love. By the grace of God, at that critical moment on May 5, He gave me repentance, and I gave Him my heart.

Peace came. Throughout the Minor Prophets, this is the promise of repentance. Repent, and God will bring mercy. Ignore the Holy One at your own risk. On Friday night I went back to Bob and Darlene's drained but encouraged, and God gave me sleep—somewhat broken, but it was sleep. Peace is a product of repentance.

For many years, falling asleep has been a challenge for me. I told people that I had trouble "turning off my brain." I would lie fully awake for hours with my mind racing from thought to thought, problem to problem, and plan to plan. Before May 3, 2017, my habit had been to take melatonin, valerian, and even Sleepy Time Tea before bed. Suzanne and I had kept strict rules about what we would discuss or do in the hours before bedtime so that my brain could shut down. May 2, 2017, was the last time I took a sleep aid. Now I get in bed, lie down, and go to sleep. I now have peace with God that had been missing for decades.

HOPEFUL HELPS

- Repentance is the first step in transformation.
- Repentance is a gift from God.
- Repentance brings peace.
- While repentance includes deep sorrow for what one has done, repentance is not grief for what one has lost.
- Read good books and watch helpful videos.
- Listen to good, godly, uplifting music for a healthy spirit.
- Beware of pride.

Starting Over

On Saturday, May 6, I continued about the business of life. I brought my clothes home from the Weers and moved into the guest room at my house. I did not sleep in the bed I had shared with Suzanne since I had last slept there with her. If I ever slept in that bed again, it would only be next to my now estranged wife. Sigh.

That same day Pastor Wilkerson called to check on me and to offer more spiritual guidance. He warned me that many times women in Suzanne's position went to the courts to seek restraining orders. He said that some of them prohibited any type of contact. He hoped that Suzanne would not take such an action, but advised me to prepare for such an outcome. I asked if he had spoken to her on the subject, but he had not.

That afternoon my son and his lovely bride came by for lunch. Nothing in the world is as precious as the love of family. The weight of the day was borne on the shoulders of two loving (adult) kids. They brought treats, including an abundance of wonderful food. My daughter-in-law knows where to shop, and she only buys the best. The food would go into the pantry and the freezer, but their visit would go into my heart to warm it against the raging blizzard of guilt. Thank You, Father, for the love of my kids!

My son warned me that a restraining order would be coming. He had asked Suzanne not to file one, telling her that "no bogeyman would ever head to Maine to hurt anyone." However, his opinion was not the one that would carry the day. My son told me that Suzanne had filed for the order on Saturday, May 6. He said that she had called him after leaving the courthouse and had read him the text. The order was going to forbid contact.

My son assured me that his mother could rescind the order at any time before the court hearing. He and my daughter-in-law repeatedly used the words *any time*. In the weeks to follow, everyone who spoke to me about the court order would stress the same thought: Suzanne needed to take this step for her own comfort. She could revoke it at will at any time before the court hearing.

My heart was crushed, yet resolute. I was the proverbial termite in a yo-yo. In my mind Suzanne's words in her letter and the words others had conveyed to me were words of reconciliation, but I saw the restraining order—especially THIS restraining order—as an act of separation, even divorce. I knew that if such an order really existed, I would be locked down. I only had a short time to say anything I might want to say.

I had a box of gifts prepared that I wanted the kids to give to Suzanne. In it was the dress, the chocolates, and a couple of other gifts I had purchased for her while I was on my way to the airport to come home from the Florida conference. I even added a sweet personal note. The kids officially knew where their mother was, but I knew, too. Suzanne had told me shortly before she left that if anything ever happened to me or if she needed to get away, she would go to her baby sister's house. I knew without "knowing" where she was.

After the kids left, Pastor Wilkerson came by for a quick visit. He suggested that I show my wife that money was not a barrier between us. I used "Quick Pay" to send a couple hundred dollars to the kids and asked them to add that to the box with a note of explanation.

The last time I had shaved my face was to come home to a woman who liked to kiss soft cheeks. If I ever shaved my face again, I decided it would be for her. My journal entry for the day concluded with these words: "I am not worthy of another chance, but my heart is fixed. I will submit to the mighty Spirit of God, and I will be the man she needs...if I ever get another chance...if."

One glimpse at a time, the LORD revealed my new life to me. I grabbed a stack of 5x7 index cards and began to make lists. My philosophy card had two initial entries: "God First" and "Scripture Decides." I made lists of tasks associated with each of my responsibilities and arranged them on the kitchen table. I was laying out my life like a military campaign with objectives and territories to conquer. Whether or not Suzanne ever returned, I knew I had to become a different man. I had to become the man God had created me to be. My wife's abandonment of our marriage was the Pearl Harbor of my soul, and I was resolved to "win through to absolute victory."

I believe pausing at this point would be worthwhile to say that I am not first or foremost a family man; I belong to God. In his excellent book, *The Exemplary Husband*, Stuart Scott reminds readers that "The most important commitment for a Christian husband is to have a heart of worship toward God alone." Making a wife into an idol defeats more than the purpose of marriage; it defeats the purpose of life.

The Reformers Unanimous addiction program focuses and builds on ten core principles. Number nine states that "We lose our freedom to choose when we give in to temptation. Our consequences are inevitable and incalculable and up to God." (Curington, 2010) After nearly thirty years of egregious sin, the extent of my consequences were now in the hands of God, but so was I. His mercies are new every morning; great is His faithfulness. With or without my wife, I had God, Who would always be enough, and my time to learn that had come.

Sunday was a mixed bag. Part was quite rough, and part was quite blessed. I rose at 3:35 a.m. without the need of an alarm clock and spent time walking with God. I prayed fervently, and I read my Bible, starting in the book of Romans. According to my journal, Chapter Six "crushed my heart with the weight of my own sin." From there I took a three-mile walk. The sun rose at 5:38 a.m. as I was on my way back to the house. I watched the stars as I meandered on paths Suzanne and I had once walked together, and I wept. I begged God to bless the girl of my dreams and to restore us. Stories varied, so I did not know exactly where she was, but I knew that she was somewhere under those same stars, probably still asleep.

The world was a different place, and I was alone in it. I was alone and frail. I was beginning to comprehend the destructive wake of my sin. If I live and study for a hundred years, I will never understand the ways in which I hurt Suzanne. I cannot. I did see through the sunrise, though, that I had hurt her enough to drive her away from home.

I was an emotional wreck under the weight of my sin and in the midst of the consuming grief of having lost my wife. For nearly thirty-eight years, I had been faithful in church, but the thought of answering people about Suzanne's absence or looking at the choir to see her missing was more than I could bear. I struggled with what to do and then decided to attend a church pastored by an old friend.

Repentance is not something easily described. I had hurt Suzanne for thirty years, and the memories are innumerable. On the drive home from church, I was overcome with waves of grief as I realized much of the harm I had engineered by causing my wife to live in fear. I relived the paralyzed looks of shattered fright in her eyes. I pictured her actually trembling with fear as tears streamed down my face, forcing me to pull the car over to weep.

At home I went again to kneel by the bed and seek God while weeping uncontrollably. Inasmuch as I had done it unto His precious daughter, I had done it unto the LORD. Memory after memory, crime after crime, hurt after hurt marched across the battlefield of my mind. I sobbed, wept, and cried out to God again and again.

Repentance is acknowledging the truth and turning from flesh to faith.

•   Jesus is THE Truth (John 14:6).

•   John 8:31-34, *Then said Jesus to those Jews which believed on him, If ye continue in my word, then are ye my disciples indeed; and ye shall know the truth, and the truth shall make you free. They answered him, We be Abraham's seed, and were never in bondage to any man: how sayest thou, Ye shall be made free? Jesus answered them, Verily, verily, I say unto you, Whosoever committeth sin is the servant of sin.* The truth makes us free.

•   John 6:63, *It is the spirit that quickeneth; the flesh profiteth nothing: the words that I speak unto you, they are spirit, and they are life.*

•   II Timothy 2:24-26, *And the servant of the LORD must not strive; but be gentle unto all men, apt to teach, patient, in meekness instructing those that oppose themselves; if God peradventure will give them repentance to the acknowledging of the truth; and that they may recover themselves out of the snare of the devil, who are taken captive by him at his will.*

As those earliest days trudged on, I kept Suzanne's phone with me at all times. Her friends were increasing their texts, asking where she was. Two of Suzanne's closest friends, Bonnie and Ruth, were asking her, "Is something wrong?"

We had known Dean and Bonnie for more than a quarter of a century. Twice our families had gone on vacations together. We had been constant companions for holidays, birthdays, and graduations. For many years we had always been with the Dean, Bonnie, Mark, and Missy as a group; our three families were almost like one. At one point several years earlier, we had started to drift, but Bonnie had remained Suzanne's sister away from home. They were the very best of friends, but the text showed that even Bonnie was clueless as to Suzanne's whereabouts.

Around mid-afternoon, another text came in from Bonnie, and I responded by calling her back and telling the truth.

"Bonnie, this is Jim. Suzanne left."

"Suzanne left what?"

"She left me. She's gone."

"You're kidding!" an astounded Bonnie replied. (Just about everyone I told from that point on would say the same words.)

In sobs I responded, "No. She left me. She's gone."

Because of the emotional turmoil of answering questions, I could not yet bear to go back to my church. I knew everyone would ask the same questions. After church I would have a conversation similar to the one I had with Bonnie with a girl named Ruth whom Suzanne had mentored as she recovered her life from a series of challenges. For months Suzanne and Ruth had been buddies, but now her mentor had vanished into thin air with a horror story for a reason.

Somewhere in the afternoon, I fell asleep. That evening I watched the church service via Internet and wondered what the future would hold. My wife was missing, I had resigned from every ministry, and I had no plan.

The Weers stopped by for a few minutes after the service to check in on me. A kind of comfort can be found in human company that can be found nowhere else. I was moving into the realm of constant loneliness, so every moment with other people would become precious. Time with Bob and Darlene was all the more precious.

On Monday I rose without an alarm clock at 3:35 a.m. to start what would become my regular routine. I threw my pillows on the floor beside the bed, took a kneeling position, and began a season of prayer.

There is no Christian life without prayer. It is our escape. It is our path to the mercy and grace that helps us in our times of need. (Hebrews 4:16) To be a Christian is to be one with Christ. For this the Master prayed,

Neither pray I for these alone, but for them also which shall believe on me through their word; that they all may be one; as thou, Father, art in me, and I in thee, that they also may be one in us: that the world may believe that thou hast sent me. And the glory which thou gavest me I have given them; that they may be one, even as we are one: I in them, and thou in me, that they may be made perfect in one; and that the world may know that thou hast sent me, and hast loved them, as thou hast loved me. (John 17:20-23)

While I realize that great men have written entire treatises on prayer, I have included these words with the hope of helping others who have fallen into a similar snare or have been hurt in similar ways. Prayer is THE grace that has redeemed my life. Prayer is what sustains me. This is WHY the LORD brought me through the valley of my despair. Compared to its importance, this topic will be brief, but please indulge me a few paragraphs to describe my beginner's approach to a walk with God.

My prayer time continues to this day and nearly always follows the same pattern. After reading (and at that time journaling) the Scripture, I start by singing to the LORD. (He is the ONLY One to Whom it sounds good.) I have a hymn book and a list of 20 songs that are written to be sung TO the LORD. Most songs in our hymnal are about the LORD, but I start with a song to Him.

My favorite song which I sing nearly every morning is taken from Psalm 139 and was put to music by Mrs. Zaida Torres.

How precious also are thy thoughts unto me, O God! How great is the sum of them! If I should count them, they are more in number than the sand: when I awake, I am still with thee.

Search me, O God, and know my heart: try me, and know my thoughts: and see if there be any wicked way in me, and lead me in the way everlasting. (vv. 17, 18, 23, 24)

The theme of another favorite, which is also taken from a Scripture, is "As the Deer" by Martin J. Nystrom. I love the way Psalm 42:1 relates to my need to desire God. *As the hart panteth after the water brooks, so panteth my soul after thee, O God.* Other songs on my list that I often sing include, "Have Thine Own Way," "Holy, Holy, Holy," and "I Surrender All."

After singing, one might begin to use the LORD's Prayer as an outline in this manner:

- *Our Father which art in heaven*

We need a Father/son relationship with God. WE need to come to Him, knowing that He loves us and that we need to love Him in return. Time with my father on this earth is not about asking him to give me what I want, but rather about each enjoying the other's presence. So should it be with our Heavenly Father.

- *Hallowed be thy name.*

One can start here by recognizing who God is. Psalm 8:1, 3-4 is a good model:

O LORD, our LORD, how excellent is thy name in all the earth! who hast set thy glory above the heavens... When I consider thy heavens, the work of thy fingers, the moon and the stars, which thou hast ordained; what is man, that thou art mindful of him? and the son of man, that thou visitest him?

Several times a year, one might do well to visualize what the psalmist meant. See yourself kneeling alone by the bed. Step up and see the smallness of your house in the neighborhood. You can then imagine the smallness of your neighborhood in the city. Is your city hard to spot with a view of the state? Is your state truly large in the country? From space, the United States is very small, but our Earth could fit 1,300,000 times in the Sun. Our star can fit many thousands of times into larger stars of which there are billions in our galaxy. The Milky Way is one galaxy among thousands, and our LORD has set His glory above those heavens.

And yet…and yet, He knows every thought of every head and numbers the hairs of every head. You are one of nearly 7.5 billion people, yet He knows your name and loves you enough that His thoughts toward you are precious. You are talking to HIM. This is prayer.

As you kneel, you might begin by honoring His name with words similar to these: "Father, You are amazing. You are wonderful. You are my Counselor, and my everlasting Father. I need You to be my Father today." Go on from there for a few minutes telling Him what He means to you.

• *Thy kingdom come*

You can relate this phrase to a relationship with the Heavenly Father. We are to rule with Him in His kingdom. Perhaps this relationship could be better understood as the family business, "Jehovah and Sons." Our elder Brother runs the shop, and everything we do, we do the Father's way.

With thanks to Clint Caviness teaching the relationship between "Thy kingdom come" in the Lord's Prayer and Romans 14, I am reminded that…

…the kingdom of God is not meat and drink; but righteousness, and peace, and joy in the Holy Ghost. For he that in these things serveth Christ is acceptable to God, and approved of men. Let us therefore follow after the things which make for peace, and things wherewith one may edify another. (Romans 14:17-19)

Here it is good to acknowledge that our only righteousness belongs to Christ, and it is good to ask Him to give us personal righteousness so that we might be clean vessels, fit to serve the Master, worthy of the family name as a good representative of "Jehovah and Sons."

You might then go on to ask Jesus for the peace that He promised to leave us in John 14. Ask for peace to still your heart for living and for peace that might flow through you to be a blessing to others. Our elder

Brother went about doing good, and as He has shown us, we need to show others the way of peace.

From there it is fitting ask the Holy Ghost to fill you with His joy. I believe Suzanne may be the best example of that joy I have ever known, and I often ask Him to fill me with joy as He fills her. We may selfishly want joy, but I also ask that the LORD would give me joy that I might spread it to those He loves.

Things wherewith one may edify another is also part of our kingdom. We are royalty— a royal priesthood. We build each other up; it's what our family does.

- *Thy will be done in earth, as it is in heaven.*

At this point I ask the LORD to show me what He wants me to do, and I ask Him to help me do it. I seek my marching orders for the day. I want Him to show me my job so that I might do it well.

- *Give us this day our daily bread.*

I am a fat, spoiled American. I have far more than daily bread in my cupboards and refrigerator, so I acknowledge that everything I have comes from Him, and I ask the LORD to bless me at work and to continue providing our needs.

- *And forgive us our debts,*

Here is where I confess my sins, though I often struggle. I try to confess sin as I am aware of it, and I often find myself unaware of a specific problem I need to confess. Again, the Scripture is my guide, and I frequently remind myself that Jesus said the two greatest commandments were to love the LORD with all of my heart, soul, and might and then to love my neighbor as myself. I fail miserably in following both of these commands every day; thus I have failed all of the commands of God.

- *As we forgive our debtors.*

Now it is time to ask the LORD to forgive those who have offended me. I ask Him to forgive them the way He forgave those who crucified Jesus when the Master said, *Father, forgive them, for they know not what they do.* (Luke 23:34) Few traits reveal my sinful nature better than the fact that I often have several names to name here.

- *And lead us not into temptation, but deliver us from evil:*

I do not understand spiritual warfare. The dueling angels of Daniel 10 make no sense to me whatsoever, but I am compelled to acknowledge that Satan's presence, purpose, and methodology in this world are taught in the

Scripture. I know that the Evil One is wont to tempt not only me, but also others around me in an attempt to steal, kill, and destroy. I take a cue from Satan's frustration in Job 1:10, where he whines to God about Job's saying, *Hast not thou made an hedge about him, and about his house, and about all that he hath on every side?* THIS is what I want and what I ask for.

I often spend more time on this one aspect of my prayer life than on any other, with the possible exception of thanksgiving. More about thanksgiving later.

Because he begged God to keep him from evil, I insert the prayer of Jabez (I Chronicles 4) into my outline at this point. I would note that Jabez was *"more honourable than his brethren."* I do not pretend to be more honorable than anyone, but God recorded his prayer, and while my understanding may be lacking, I use it.

- *Oh that thou wouldest bless me indeed*

The first two points of the prayer of Jabez get a bit muddled in my prayer room. I do ask the LORD to make it abundantly clear to me and everyone else that HE has blessed my life. I ask Him to bless me in big, obvious ways.

- *And enlarge my coast*

I ask God to give me more of everything—more wisdom, more wealth, more influence, better health, and more of every other good and perfect gift. I delight in the fact that God is no respecter of persons and that He can hear my prayer like He did that of Jabez. I do, however, qualify this request based upon Proverbs 30:8-9a, *Remove far from me vanity and lies: give me neither poverty nor riches; feed me with food convenient for me: lest I be full, and deny thee, and say, Who is the LORD?*

In asking God to bless me abundantly in every conceivable way, I remind Him that HE is Who and What I need. I ask Him to give me only that which He knows I will give back to Him. I do not want to be as Solomon who turned the blessings of God into idolatry and debauchery.

- *And that thine hand might be with me*

While faith is not feeling, I want to know the presence of God in my life. I want to stay aware of Him—Who He is and what He does.

- *And that thou wouldest keep me from evil, that it may not grieve me!*

This is the line that caused me to put the prayer of Jabez into my outline at this point.

- *For thine is the kingdom, and the power, and the glory, for ever.*

I close the preamble to my prayer time with an acknowledgment that God is sovereign. All I have belongs to Him. After this, I begin with my list of people and ideas for which I pray. I start with asking God for wisdom and love, and then I pray for the needs in Suzanne's life.

Because I gave my wife 10,898 days of a living Hell, I asked the LORD to reunite us and to give us more than 11,000 days of love, grace, and respect. From this point, I pray for our kids, other people, ministries, and prayer requests that I have accepted from friends.

HOPEFUL HELPS

- Pray.
- Sing.
- Repent.
- Beware of pride.

Digging In

In her letter Suzanne had written, "It is my longing and desire that you seek professional and spiritual help for your medical and spiritual issues…" Medical issues mattered, so on Sunday, May 7, I began journaling my pain. On the doctors' scale of 1-10, I was still experiencing many days of 7 to 9; every day was a perpetual state of 3 to 4. The pain in the ENTIRE left side from my buttocks to my toes was agonizing and chronic. Gabapentin and Tramadol helped, but I was always in considerable pain. On most nights I was still adding Tylenol 3 to alleviate the pain so I could sleep. On Monday I called for an appointment with my primary care physician and was scheduled to see her on Wednesday. At the appointment, I told her everything and let her know that I had to find answers to my questions about drug interactions. "Doctor, I have to find ways to better manage my pain."

Suzanne had asked me to seek professional counseling, so I also arranged weekly sessions with a Christian psychotherapist named Steve. Because of perceptions from childhood and because of teaching I had received early in my adulthood, I had deep-rooted suspicions regarding psychotherapy. I was not sure what to think of or expect from Steve. He and I have had interesting appointments through our season of counseling.

On Tuesday I had my first appointment with my therapist. Point by point, I was completely committed. Suzanne had been God's effective channel for humbling me, and she had kindly painted the picture of where I needed to begin the next phase of healing. Through the details of her letter she had laid out the pieces of my puzzle. Sometimes love does the hard thing; sometimes love hurts, but love has godly intentions for its object. Thank God for love.

The LORD reminded me that in the multitude of counselors, there is safety. I cannot thank God enough for Pastor Wilkerson, as he met with me daily at first and helped me set up so many aspects of my life. My pastor is not the kind of counselor to push himself on someone or to take an authoritative position, but he is very adept at gently guiding people to see the truth of God's Word. As he and I graduated from the initial crisis and the daily contact, I scheduled weekly appointments with him. I appointed my pastor as the chief architect in helping me redesign my spiritual life.

I knew certain issues needed to be removed from my life. With the hope that I would someday have a restored marriage, I also wanted to look for qualities I need to add into my marriage. I also chose to counsel with Pastor Bob, one of the pastors of Christway Baptist Church in Dyer, Indiana. Bob may be the best Bible teacher I have ever known. He is very good at helping people understand God's truths, and he has a humble spirit that I would do well to emulate. I chose Pastor Bob to help me prepare for a new marriage.

I also needed a counselor as a sounding board. The heart is deceitful above all things and desperately wicked, so the notion of trusting my heart was out. I chose my longtime friend and West Virginia pastor, Craig, to listen to and help me correct my thinking. After making these choices, I had four counselors every week as well as a group of medical experts to help guide me.

Isolation is a strange place to live. My wife and nearly all of the family associated with her had cut off contact entirely. My daughter was not yet ready to speak to me, and my son was immersed in the early successes of a new career. Days were indescribably long, though also extremely full.

At 9:56 a.m. on May 9, I received a text message from Suzanne's brother. The text message said that my wife was "…in a safe place with very supportive assistance. She is seeking professional and legal help for victims of domestic violence."

He did not define the term "legal help" and did not answer my questions about the wording. Divorce was the only legal option I could imagine, as I had not touched anyone in anger for nearly eight years at that time. He told me to focus on myself—not on Suzanne or our marriage. I was completely unable to make sense of the many different currents of information, and I found myself trying to put the different thoughts into context. My brother-in-law was speaking from a vantage point I did not fully understand. I pondered, "What exactly DID 'legal help' mean?"

Despite the strong foreshadowing from my wife's brother, and though May 9 marked only the sixth day since Suzanne had left, I had begun to think that my son was wrong. I began to think and hope that she had not filed for a protection order. (In Maine, these are known as "Protection from Abuse" orders or PFAs. In other states, other names and acronyms are used.)The police had not shown up, and I had assumed that they would arrive the day after she filed the order. As it turned out, I learned interstate legal matters did not work that way. This particular ignorance was a short-lived bliss.

So as to avoid the appearance of manipulation that might come with a lavish gift, I ordered Suzanne a small, cross-shaped plaque for her birthday and addressed it to be delivered at her baby sister's house. I was enthused that the order was not going through, and I had high hopes to hear from my wife soon. I continued writing email messages and sending them into oblivion.

May 10 was Suzanne's birthday. I truly hoped to hear from her. Though attempts were made to block me from Facebook, it IS social media, and I did see that she had a party. Lots of family members attended to her, and she had a great-looking cake. She looked happy—very happy—but she did not call. She had presents, but I did not see the plaque I sent in the pictures. As it turned out, Amazon was late, and my present would not be delivered until the next day.

On May 11, I arrived at home to find the protection order rubber banded to the doorknob. The order was illegible, so I texted my brother-in-law to ask for a legible copy. He emailed it, and I opened it. My heart sank.

The protection order forbade ANY contact—direct or indirect. Had I asked someone to tell Suzanne that I loved her, I would have been eligible for jail and a large fine. The order required counseling, prohibited me from possessing any firearms, and would request financial support after the hearing.

More than all of that, in Suzanne's own handwriting were the stark details of many of the worst crimes I had commited. For several pages, she outlined exactly what kind of monster I had been. My blood ran cold. How could any human commit such acts against any other human? Horror, dread, guilt, shame, self-loathing, and anguish swirled in a raging vortex that sucked me deeper yet into the murky abyss of despair. I could not read it, but I could not help but read it. I wept and prayed and confessed, but why should God hear such a fiend as I?

Her words, of course, were just the tip of the proverbial iceberg. Across the miles, Suzanne and I both knew that I had committed many more heinous acts than could be jotted on a notebook in a courthouse. Day after day for the first several years of our marriage and then again at intervals for all of the remaining years, I had treated my wife horrifically. I was only beginning to learn the damage I had done on this side of eternity. That I will ever know the true depths of my own depravity is unlikely. Even one story given in full detail would render this book unreadably horrible. What was such a man as I to do?

He that walketh with wise men shall be wise, so I delved deeply into books. In the first forty days, I read ten books. In my entire library, only one book was completely secular. The *Slight Edge* by Jeff Olson is a worthwhile addition to any library about the momentum of repeating right behaviors. Every other book or video was written from a Christian perspective. Over the next few months, my stack of resource books would be over a foot tall. Of course, I also spent hours every week in my Bible.

Reconciling the deep grief in my heart for the hurt I had caused my wife with the fact that I was the person who had committed all of those awful acts is impossible. The blinders came off, and I caught a glimpse of the wasteland of destruction I now knew thirty years could cause. Sadly, there is no way for a perpetrator to ever truly empathize with a victim. When a person gives the helm of his soul to pride or rage or anger or to any of the legion of despotic demons, he loses his grasp on what he is doing. Such a person commits crimes that pass effortlessly through his own memory while creating an indelible imprint on the mind of the innocent.

However accurate or weak my memories were, they came into focus as I confessed. Grief became my universe, my vision, and my future. I would have given my life to go back and undo my evil deeds, but God does not grant do-overs in this world. Repentance became an all-consuming force.

Over time I would have to learn that the only person qualified to forgive me was Christ Himself. The Lamb slain before the foundation of the world has grace that is greater than my need. He was ready for me, and in time I would learn to accept His grace.

As soon as I began to make my confession before the LORD, I also began sending conciliatory messages to the email address I had discovered during the wee hours of May 4. I had no idea how obsessive they were. I had no idea if she would ever read them.

These messages will read differently to every reader. One cannot put tone of voice or body language into text. Nevertheless, they do show a bit of my heart.

5/5

Good morning.

I love you.

I spent a mostly sleepless night at the Weers'. They came to the house worried about you and found two boxes of Kleenex and a roll of paper towels full of my tears.

They called Pastor Wilkerson. All agreed I should not spend the night alone, so the Weers took me to their house.

They know you are gone and how I behaved on the 14th-17th.

I love you more than you can ever understand.

Jim

Prayed fervently for you today.

♥♥♥♥♥

I love you.

These will be my counselors: (counselors' website). They were recommended by Pastor Wilkerson.

I went through a multi-stage application with Blue Cross today, and they rejected me. I will pay cash.

I requested an appointment but do not yet have a date.

I love you.

♥♥♥♥♥

May 6

Good morning.

I love you.

I am walking with God and have prayed for you.

God gave me sleep last night, and that was very helpful.

Suzanne,

I had said that I would send you three messages a day, but yesterday evening the pastor (copied on this message) was concerned that this may be too much. I showed him the texts of three messages, and he was of a slightly different opinion because he did not see me trying to manipulate you. (Brother John, you are free to comment for yourself, and you do not have to copy me on such a comment.)

I am going to slow down significantly for now. I will limit myself to one message a day at most and will continue the same tone (NOT the tone of that very first message). In doing so, please allow me these observations:

- Your letter said, "I WANT to talk to you."
- That gave me hope.
- I understand your reticence to be on the phone with me.
- I know I need help, and as my notes have said, I am seeking it.
- I am making no attempt to find you; if you were with (a friend) in Munster, I

would not go there. I am not interested in coercing you.

- It is very hard to say this, but I do not believe you should be with me right now.
- I have not used terms of endearment or pet names because I am trying to avoid my control-freak side; please understand that the affection is there, just waiting for your permission.
- Please consider opening the lines of communications just a crack, but immediately.

There is a component of selfishness here; there is definite benefit to me. I need hope.

If you would be so kind, please consider these thoughts:

Please forgive me for the message of 9:56 a.m. on May 4 entitled "Forward."

- I had not slept in 30 hours when I wrote it.
- I had not spoken to a person since (our friends) left.
- I had not repented before God at all.
- If you have not read it, would you please consider deleting it unread? I want to apologize with the type of words you would expect from me, but do not want to cross another line.
- Please read my messages.
- I will not try to coerce you.
- I do want help and am seeking it.
- I have volumes more to say than I have said; if you agree to read the journal, I will put much of it there.
- Please send some type of response daily.
- Just "Thanks" indicating you read the message would lift my spirits.
- If I say something that is uncomfortable or out of line, tell me, and I will work with my counselors to correct it.

I told Pastor Wilkerson that I agreed (I used stronger terms) that I need serious help and that you were the only person who could help move me there. I told him that I agreed that you needed to do something drastic to get my attention. I told him that I do not think you should come home immediately.

(Perhaps this is a sign of what truly happens in a heart at the time of repentance? I knew from the morning of May 5 that no type of return to the "old" marriage was permissible. I did not yet have the vocabulary to describe it, but I knew that IF we were ever to be together again, we had to have a born-again relationship. Old things would have to pass away; all things would need to become new.

I told several people during this time that I could not pray, *Create in me a clean heart, O God, and renew a right spirit within me*" but that I had to modify the Psalm and pray,....create *a right spirit within me*).

Though you don't come home immediately, please consider opening the lines of communication immediately. We don't have to start with phone calls, but please give me hope.

May I please make an additional request? I promise to behave and am happy to have someone monitor the calls, but please let me briefly express love to you on your birthday and Mother's Day. Please give me permission to say things that are more affectionate than I have said so far. If you do not, I will not.

I am more selfish than this closing, but I am working on it; I have made the end of it my new signature for this email account.

For God is my witness, whom I serve with my spirit in the gospel of His Son, that without ceasing I make mention of you always in my prayers; making request, if by any means now at length I might have a prosperous journey by the will of God to come unto you. For I long to see you, that I may impart unto you some spiritual gift, to the end ye may be established; that is, that I may be comforted together with you by the mutual faith both of you and me.

I love you,

Jim

That protection order carried the weight of law, and it was set to govern my relationship with Suzanne for two years after the hearing, which was set for May 26. The individual who has never walked the road of recovery from abuse might wonder why a spouse who says that she wants reconciliation would seek an order forbidding any direct or indirect contact. How does a person work on reconciliation without communication? Is communication not the first order of business in marriage seminars, retreats, and counseling? As it turns out, opening the lines of communication in the process of recovering from abuse is far more complicated.

In 1981 domestic abuse pioneers began to work on what would come to be known as the Duluth Model. While joining in the praise or criticism of the model is beyond the scope of my expertise, one must recognize that caring people gave diligence to study the topic and to build a model for "thinking about how a community works together to end domestic violence." Their wheel models are commonplace at sites seeking to help victims. At the center of the wheel are the words "Power and Control."

Most people who work to help victims of abuse consider "power and control" to be at the center of the problem and believe that open communication creates an avenue for the abuser to maintain both. Many victims of abuse question themselves, blame themselves, and seek to fix abuse problems by fixing themselves.

The short story is that a woman who has lived for years under duress needs time apart to heal and to gain a godly perspective of herself and her relationships. In the 1988 presidential campaign, Lee Atwater opined that "perception is reality." Those who loved Suzanne did not want my communications to influence her perceptions. This is, in fact, an important protection that abuse victims do need. Though I was learning, I, at that point, knew little of the healing process.

Moreover, I was not ready to meet her needs. The decades of sin had bent my soul horribly. Replacing selfish anger with godly grace would require me to spend much time alone with God. He had begun His good work in me.

HOPEFUL HELPS

- Restoration is a process.
- Healing is a process; victims of abuse need time to heal.
- Healing is a process; abusers need time to grow.
- Seek godly counsel.
- Beware of pride.

Digging Out

I did know that the consequences of my deeds had hurt me, and I had to find a way forward. As I considered my reentry into the community at First Baptist Church, I began to mull coming before the church during the invitation. Suzanne was missing, and people would wonder "Why?" I did not want HER to seem like the bad guy. Also, I had resigned all of my duties. What was I supposed to do with all of the boys in my Sunday school class? Kade had written an essay I had challenged the class to write, and he was seeking me to deliver his essay. Another boy wanted me to know who they now had as a Sunday school teacher.

The truth is that I am a part of a church family, but I had hurt them. Hypocrisy and pride pierce deeply. Church is not supposed to be the home of such cruelty. The members of our congregation deserved more than a confession, but church services have time constraints. My wife, a Sunday school teacher, a WMS leader, a choir member, a singing group coordinator, an addiction counselor, and the trusted friend of many was gone.

I spoke with Pastor Wilkerson, and he thought my confession was a good idea. I told him I would do it. I also mentioned it to the kids. They reminded me that Mother's Day fell on that Sunday and that my going forward could be somewhat awkward. Awkward would have to do. In order for me to join the congregation anew, there had to be a reckoning.

On Tuesday, May 9, the same day that my brother-in-law had told me Suzanne was seeking professional and legal counsel, I made a trip by Mark and Missy's house to find out what Missy, Suzanne's close friend, thought. Going in front of thousands of people with a public statement was bold and would involve Suzanne at a time when I could not ask her opinion. I had already learned enough in my reading to know that making such decisions without her was a part of my coercive past. I pondered, what do I do?

Missy was confident that what I planned to do was a good idea. She and Mark were great company. Who am I kidding? Anyone with a pulse who spoke English was good company to a man in my state, but these were friends of a lifetime who cared and who knew. Their encouragement buoyed my spirits immeasurably.

A few days later, I would text Missy what I intended to have the pastor read for me. An attribute of pride is to be manipulative, and the fact that I still had these thoughts was telling: I was confident that Missy would share my intentions with Suzanne. My hope was that if my wife objected, Missy would tell me. I was using Missy to communicate with Suzanne without telling her. Using people is wrong, and sometimes pride is subtle like it was in this illustration.

Just as I suspected, Missy shared my intentions with Suzanne. Word spread. From coast to coast people were ready to watch and/or record the end of the Sunday morning service.

Sunday was an emotional hurricane. I had only shared with Pastor Wilkerson and the two close friends what my intentions were. When people had asked me about Suzanne, I told them the truth. I frankly said, "My wife left me after decades of abusive anger in our home." Tears flowed like fountains, and I did what I could to avoid people.

Just before the service began, a young man I had mentored when he was in our church's addiction home, approached me. At this Mother's Day service, that young man was excited to introduce me to his mother. I do not remember his words at all, but I know that he made me out as some sort of a hero or a person of importance. I was polite but nauseous. I grieved in silence for how my confession would hurt my young friend and his mother.

As the sermon came to a close, the pastor began the invitation by inviting anyone who had never trusted Christ as Saviour to come forward. He also invited anyone who needed to pray at the altar or make spiritual decisions to come forward. I walked to the front and handed one of the altar workers a card I had already filled out. She sent it to the pastor, who already knew exactly what it said:

I am coming before the church to confess nearly 30 years of abusive anger at home. I am seeking the LORD and want to be the man He can lead me to become. Suzanne is away for now seeking help and healing.

I cried like a baby, but it was neither the first nor the last time. Grief flooded back over me anew as I wondered if this public confession of sin would hurt or help Suzanne. I wondered what it would do for my kids. I wondered almost endlessly. I was ashamed and relieved. I was anguished, and then I was surprised.

"Jim, that took guts," said one person. "I'm going to pray for you every day," I heard from many. Several promised to have me over for a meal.

Person after person came to offer me love. Did they not hear? I was the monster in a horror story. I was the bad guy. This whole situation was my fault, and she was the innocent one. They knew, but love and support flowed like twin rivers of grace. I would not know it for a long time, but publicly confessing my sin was one of the best decisions I had ever made.

Brethren, if a man be overtaken in a fault, ye which are spiritual, restore such an one in the spirit of meekness; considering thyself, lest thou also be tempted. Bear ye one another's burdens, and so fulfil the law of Christ. For if a man think himself to be something, when he is nothing, he deceiveth himself. (Galatians 6:1-3)

At this point in my journey, people began to do their part in the work of my restoration. Here are a few:

Wayne invited me to start exercising with him daily at Planet Fitness. Wayne, even with his growing enterprise, and the fact that he never stops working, made time. He has a goal of giving millions of dollars to the LORD's work every year, and he is about that business day and night. For him to drive from his office in the opposite direction of his home to meet me for 30 to 45 minutes of exercise was not reasonable, but he did—time and again. When Wayne traveled, he had me take him to and from the airports. Somehow he knew that one of my greatest needs was a break in the solitude.

Deacon Jon, is one of the most faithful servants in my church. He has spent decades in the bus ministry, teaching men and ladies in Sunday school, and greeting and serving as a deacon. His family serves with him, and he gives his life to his LORD with his family. Jon started giving me his Saturdays. First, he took me out to lunch and heard my story (God bless him!). Then Saturday after Saturday, he took me soul winning and visiting his converts.

Bob and Darlene were the angels from Heaven who had rescued me on May 4, but they never stopped giving themselves to me. Bob either met me or called me nightly to pray. We spent 30 minutes to an hour every night together. The Weers also invited me to stay at their house as often as I wished, and they fed me every time. Soon we settled on Saturday nights. Each Saturday evening, I made my way to their home to live for one night a week as a member of a family.

And there were more:

• A couple who had known Suzanne and me for decades invited me over for lunch.

- Josh offered to take me to lunch any time I wanted to and to be available to listen. One day we spoke for nearly an hour.

- Steve and Laurie have more than they can say grace over. Laurie is diabetic and has suffered through two strokes; Steve works to be Dad and a fill-in for Mom while providing and managing the family. They invited me for a Sunday dinner.

- The pastor's wife, Linda, had me over for lunch on a Sunday while their house was full of servants of God.

- Elton is the chairman of our deacons. He and his wife spent a long evening with me at a restaurant, explaining a Christ-honoring marriage. His wife Barb sent me regular encouragements and articles on Facebook Messenger.

- Dave and Tony give their lives the Reformers Unanimous ministry at our church; they took me out for coffee after church, and Dave took me to dinner the next Sunday.

- Mark, my new Sunday school teacher now that I had resigned my class, took me to breakfast and had frequent phone calls with me. His wife, Priscilla, confidentially reached out to Suzanne and became an encouragement to her.

- Dave is the president of our church's Bible college and is one of the primary counselors at the church. His wife works in the real estate business and volunteers extensively with our youth. They have their own adult Sunday school class. They came over and spent an evening encouraging me.

- Paul works more than full time managing the cleanliness of the dozens of buildings on our church campus. He also volunteers extensively with our addiction and homeless ministries and our radio station. He came over multiple times to encourage me.

- Pat knew me as a teenager and became a prayer partner. She spent two long phone calls encouraging me.

- Dave and his wife Linda have known my wife and me since we were teenagers. They frequently offered me bold encouragement, saying that they actually respected me for my public confession. They spent an evening at the house looking at my work and offering me encouragement.

- Larry sought me out at nearly every church service to tell me that the LORD was my comfort and that I could keep going.

- Doug sought me out at nearly every church service to inquire of my welfare and to offer encouragement.

- Kade, who had been in my Sunday school class when I resigned, sought me out at nearly every church service to greet and encourage me. His parents, Kerry and Patty, were constantly kind.
- A family in our Sunday school class offered me a transparent look at their life, separation, and continued struggles.
- Robin told me in tears that she prayed for our marriage every day.
- Charlie and Glenda had me over to their house for a home-cooked dinner and told me about how the love worked in their marriage.

The stories of the goodness of God's people are too many to remember and too numerous to tell.

As I have mentioned, word reached those in Maine that I would be making this confession on May 14. In addition to having several thousand people in the live audience, a live-streaming crowd included the folks with whom Suzanne was staying. Because of time zones, they were able to record it for my wife and play it back to her when she returned home from church. The word that came back from Missy was simply that she saw it and was blessed.

Even one brother-in-law offered encouragement. On May 15 he wrote, "I believe that with God's work of healing and transformation in your life, in time, He may very well use you in a major way to minister to others who struggle with the same anger and abuse issues. Moment by moment, day by day, may we (you and me) be men who truly lead...by being a reflection/mirror of Christ's love, grace, forgiveness, and compassion."

The LORD instructs His own through Solomon that *He that covereth his sins shall not prosper: but whoso confesseth and forsaketh them shall have mercy.* (Proverbs 28:13). Mercy beyond measure was what poured into my life after that public confession. I had not confessed to seek mercy; my goals had been to protect Suzanne's name and to clear the air for my reentry into the church family. The twin rivers of love and support flowed around me, creating a moat of grace around the castle of my restoration. The public confession of my guilt had become the best decision I would make. Thanks be to God.

Almost immediately after Suzanne left, I began to journal. I cannot explain why, but somehow I knew that this part of my life needed to be recorded. Usually I would record some of the daily events, a bit of my Bible reading, and some of my feelings. After the protection order took place, I also wrote brief notes to Suzanne. On Monday, May 15, I simply recorded some verses that had spoken to me that morning.

Romans 15:1-4, *We then that are strong ought to bear the infirmities of the weak, and not to please ourselves. Let every one of us please his neighbor for his good to edification. For even Christ pleased not himself; but, as it is written, The reproaches of them that reproached thee fell on me...that we through patience and comfort of the scriptures might have hope...*

God makes us likeminded. Verse 5 says, Now the God of patience and consolation grant you to be likeminded one toward another according to Christ Jesus... Verse 13 continues, Now the God of hope fill you with all joy and peace in believing, that ye may abound in hope, through the power of the Holy Ghost.

As the days ticked by, that there would be no change before May 26 became apparent. Both family members and others who were communicating with Suzanne had several observations. They believed that loved ones were exerting strong influence over my wife's choices; they believed that she was looking forward to the hearing date being past as a step toward the next steps.

I had not read the temporary order correctly. In a conversation with Suzanne's brother on May 15, he told me that the State of Maine provided spousal support and that Suzanne had an excellent lawyer with much experience representing abuse victims. He began to urge me not to attend the court hearing. I began to feel quite threatened by his words and tone, and I reached out to a lawyer in the town where the hearing would take place.

Jesus is our advocate in Heaven, but I had never understood the term quite so clearly before. Rebecca, a family lawyer in Topsham, Maine, is an advocate. In my letter to her I made it very clear that I was the "bad guy" in the story. A couple of days later I would send her a copy of the court order along with this introduction:

Rebecca,

Attached is the order.

On a personal note, I know that the legal system recognizes a need for everyone to be represented. I also assume by your bio that you have represented a lot of women who have been victims in cases like this, and there must be a corresponding distaste for representing one of the bad guys.

I am one of the bad guys. I am guilty as accused in this order.

Please know that I am absolutely consumed with my own rehabilitation. I am taking every step with every counselor and reading every book with the intent of seeing God change me completely. I want to give Suzanne what she deserved 30 years ago. She lived in fear for 10,898 days. It is my passion to give her 11,000 days of love, respect, and blessing. I am giving every waking moment to it.

For legal matters, here are documentable steps I have taken...

(I outlined steps already listed above and closed.)

I think that is the summary.

Rebecca started seeking my benefit and protection immediately. She sought not only to protect me against all comers, but she also sought to protect me against myself. Her responses were timely, clear, and effective. She fought for me as one would fight for the "good guy" in such a story. Of note, her firm handles many domestic cases, and no doubt, she has represented abused women. For a credentialed professional with such experience to look down with disgust on one such as I would be easy. She was respectful, thorough, and professional. I have never met her face-to-face, but I thank God for that young lady. If nine out of ten lawyers give the "others" a bad name, then Rebecca is one of the "others."

My routine continued. I always woke before the alarm, sometime between 3:00 and 4:00 a.m. I would greet the LORD, turn on the light, make the bed, set my pillows, and drop to my knees for prayer. After prayer I would dress quickly, blend a salad for lunch, and leave for work. It became my habit to be at the office by 6:00; consequently, I would leave shortly after 2:00.

I stopped spending money. If I wanted to love my bride the way Christ loved His bride, I would need to prepare a place for her. Since I had no way to express my love to Suzanne with words, I had begun just days after she left to express love with my hands. Except to prepare a place for her, I stopped spending money almost altogether.

First, I emptied the front room. I even moved the piano up the single stair step into the kitchen and then moved it to the dining room by myself. The flooring in that room was peel-and-stick vinyl tile that was wearing through to show the 1950s-era linoleum. For my first project, I laid a new laminate Pergo™-style floor and repainted the trim and door. Next I went to the back of the house and painted over the very last of the dark wood paneling in the house. I painted it the color Suzanne had wanted.

Over the course of the next twenty weeks, I would go on to replace the floors in the master bedroom and the kitchen. I also tiled the entire bathroom, tub, and floor with ceramic tile (I needed a little help from my friend Mark on that part of the project.) Our bedroom had been wainscoted in bright red. Because red is an angry color, I repainted the lower section with a seascape green.

On May 16 at my second appointment with Steve, he was full of questions. "What?" "Why?" "How did you feel?" He wanted me to tell him at the next appointment what I saw in all of the books I was reading. The simple fact was that I was beginning to see the world as a battleground. On one side was an abusive, manipulative, selfish monster of an ego. On the other side was love, family, and faith. Pride vs faith was the story of my world. I saw it played out everywhere. Life was an epic battle of my flesh against His Spirit.

May 26, a red-letter date on my calendar, was the date appointed by the court to consider granting a permanent (2-year) order of protection. I would see Suzanne in court, and she would see me. I knew that God was making huge changes in my life, and I hoped that she would be able to see a visible change in me. I hoped that my offers would make sense to her and that we would be able to begin communicating. That date was a day of dread and a day of hope.

I knew that God was moving in my life, and I had high hopes for a speedy reunion. I had begun to ask people to pray that we could be back together by our thirtieth anniversary, July 2. Day by day, prayer time was a piece of Heaven, and night by night, estranged separation was a stay in Hell. Memories were the mesh that held them together.

HOPEFUL HELPS

- Humility is required for repentance and for restoration.
- True restoration is a team effort; we need each other desperately.
- Beware of pride.

Digging Up

On my way to catch a commuter train in Chicago one afternoon, I called Mom to ask questions about my anger. "When did it begin?" "How did it happen?" My memories were vague, but with some prompting, they came back.

My parents separated when I was four, and between my parents, there have been six marriages. For many reasons I would not point to one person, a certain place, or a particular time in print, but I will reveal that I had seen domestic violence as a child. I had experienced fear that was enough to cause me to pass out more than once. I had seen periods of anger that gripped and controlled a family. Shortly after my parents' divorce, I began to have rather wild episodes of anger, but my outbursts were always at home or among my family members.

A counselor has advised me, and I have seen it referenced many times in my reading: hurt people are people who hurt people. Most men who commit domestic abuse observed it in their childhood. Given the sad but shocking prevalence of the problem, that makes some sense. We can pass these problems to our children unwittingly.

In junior high and high school, I had no flare-ups at all. Through college, I had only a couple of "isolated" events. Not until two days after our wedding did the anger I had shown in childhood truly come back. From that first tantrum, the episodes grew into daily events for many years.

Abuse was Daddy's dirty little secret. Suzanne knew, and our kids knew that the problems we had at home were to stay at home. They were no one else's business. This kind of secrecy is a common factor in abusive homes. All of the victims are indoctrinated in the importance of keeping the secret.

Lenore Walker, Ed. D., the founder of the Domestic Violence Institute, is credited with first explaining the cycle of domestic violence. She describes phases in which tension builds, battery happens, and a honeymoon follows. Since she published *The Battered Woman* in 1979, much has been written on the subject. Considerable progress has been made in establishing and providing help for women who have been victims of abuse. Certainly, much research and work on domestic violence has come about since 1979, but what Walker's work and the work of those who followed has clearly shown is that women need help, and they need to know where that help can be found.

At times in our marriage, I followed the pattern Dr. Walker described. Once, during the first months of our marriage after a horrible event, I took Suzanne out to eat at Denny's in the middle of the night. We were the picture of a honeymoon in the abuse cycle. Suzanne was convinced of my love as we shared a wonderful time of confession, contrition, and forgiveness. Sadly, men need help, too, and they need to know where to find help. I did not get it that night or any night for many years.

Somewhere in the fabric of our home, there was a hole. When the hole was covered, peace reigned; however, each time the cover came off, the blast furnace of Hell melted Suzanne's soul and poured it out like water.

Proverbs 11:29 warns, *He that troubleth his own house shall inherit the wind....* More accurate words could never be spoken. Every episode of anger and wrath had one factor in common: I was the root cause. Through a process I shall describe shortly, I created every moment of rage and fear from within. Neither Suzanne nor our children had any impact. My past did not hurt my wife, my upbringing did not hurt my children, and our church did not inflict the pain: I alone was the root. I was the trouble in our house. The wind was mine to inherit.

The terror of that realization is beyond anything Stephen King has ever written. Edgar Allan Poe could not describe the torment of a man's soul when he truly faces such facts. Truth is stronger than fiction. Help must come from somewhere. Can help come from church? That question must be answered one church at a time.

Many years earlier, Suzanne approached one of the most trusted counselors we knew. She asked if Ephesians 5:22-24 meant that if I told her she was not allowed to seek counsel about our marriage without me, she could not do so. With sadness, he instructed her that the passage meant exactly that. He did not ask if she was safe; he did not instruct her about what to do in the event of abuse. He simply gave her an answer that strengthened the chains of her enslavement.

On another occasion Suzanne took physical evidence of an awful event to a couple she trusted. She told them what had happened and asked for help. They listened intently and were very sorry, but for one reason or another, they did not want to get involved. Would you? Do you know anything about the Domestic Abuse Hotline? Do you know what position your church holds on abuse inside of marriage? Do you have an approach in mind? What do you believe the Bible says?

Women who are suffering in abusive relationships need help, and they cannot get it from people on the sidelines who are unwilling to get their hands dirty. Loving people involves risk, and loving people in trouble involves great risk. Are you willing? If so, exactly how willing are you?

Long before we met, Suzanne believed in a literal interpretation of the Bible. If one believes that the Bible is God's Word to be obeyed, can he, in good conscience, turn a deaf ear to such a cry? Is Romans 13 a warning to those who would break the law inside of a "Christian" home?

Romans 13:1-4, *Let every soul be subject unto the higher powers. For there is no power but of God: the powers that be are ordained of God. Whosoever therefore resisteth the power, resisteth the ordinance of God: and they that resist shall receive to themselves damnation. For rulers are not a terror to good works, but to the evil. Wilt thou then not be afraid of the power? do that which is good, and thou shalt have praise of the same. For he is the minister of God to thee for good. But if thou do that which is evil, be afraid; for he beareth not the sword in vain: for he is the minister of God, a revenger to execute wrath upon him that doeth evil.*

Is there an exclusion to the responsibility of the church to her members inside of a home? Jesus gave instructions.

Matthew 18:15-17, *Moreover if thy brother shall trespass against thee, go and tell him his fault between thee and him alone: if he shall hear thee, thou has gained thy brother. But if he will not hear thee, then take with thee one or two more, that in the mouth of two or three witnesses every word may be established. And if he shall neglect to hear them, tell it unto the church: but if he neglect to hear the church, let him be unto thee as a heathen man and a publican.*

In abusive relationships, one can rest assured that the abused has brought the matter to the other spouse alone. What would you do if you were asked to go as a witness to confront an abuser and to hear every word in the presence of two or three witnesses? Would you be inclined to offer protection? Would you be inclined to demand steps be taken to protect the abused? Are you willing to call law enforcement? If not, are you willing to stand by until such abuse ends in divorce or worse?

What of those who offer to counsel church members? Have today's pastors, church staff, and elders prepared themselves to understand the matter of abuse? Abuse is no more a marriage problem than child abuse is a parenting problem. Marriage problems are relationship issues. Marriage problems have no victim. They include how to discipline children, how to manage money, respect, communication, and differing ideas about intimacy. Marriage problems do not have perpetrators and victims; those are terms applied to crimes. Does your church recognize the difference?

NOTHING I ever did to my wife was the fault of my church or anyone else, but when I turned to my church in 2017, I found a different church than we found in the early years of our marriage. The church has a constitution that recognizes church discipline. That constitution is given to every new candidate for membership. We have a pastor who respected the need to protect my wife and who never once told Suzanne to come home. Family members were afraid that the pastor would tell her to return home to fix our marriage by being sweeter and more submissive. Why did they fear the possibility of Suzanne's hearing that advice? Their fears were certainly founded. Would to God that every abuse victim had an advocate in the office of pastor like Pastor Wilkerson and a defender of the faith at the head of the deacon board like Deacon Elton.

Pastor Wilkerson almost never approaches counseling without reminding himself of II Timothy 2:24-26: *And the servant of the LORD must not strive; but be gentle unto all men, apt to teach, patient, in meekness instructing those that oppose themselves; if God peradventure will give them repentance to the acknowledging of the truth; and that they may recover themselves out of the snare of the devil, who are taken captive by him at his will.*

When someone has been a victim of abuse, are you ready to be gentle? Are you ready to meet her at her need and to hear her plea? What of the abuser? Does he count as being "among all men"? Are you ready to be gentle with him? It's a tall order, but it is the scriptural approach to allowing a fallen man to recover himself from Satan's snare. The meekness of the pastor kept him from even once telling Suzanne that she should come home or from suggesting to her what her timeline should be. When court orders are sent and when family members involve themselves, one might be tempted to seek for solutions. At such times, being patient and offering instruction in meekness are both harder to do than to say, but God's way is always good, and God's way is always right.

As May 26 drew closer, my focus was on the words I had heard so many times. Suzanne could change or cancel the order of protection at any time she so desired. Once the order was issued by a judge, options would be different. At that point, it would become "permanent," and in the terms of the State of Maine, permanent meant two years after which the order could only be changed by a judge. To my way of thinking, because Suzanne had seemingly emphasized the changeability of the order, she must have intended to change it.

On May 17 I listened to a guest speaker at church. From my perspective, he spoke about America and oppression. Everything was about intimidation and fear versus love and faith. My sin was ever before me, and it came home when the service ended.

Tonya, a young lady my wife had been helping in the Reformers Unanimous ministry, walked up to me after the service and asked where Suzanne was. I thought the whole church had seen my confession, and I was unprepared for the question. Like a zombie, I blurted out a soulless answer, "She left me." Tonya burst into tears, turned from me, and walked away.

It's hard to realize how interconnected our lives are. Before Tonya was ever born, I had begun to abuse her. You may wonder, "How?" I did so by abusing her future mentor who would have to flee in fear, leaving behind the Tonyas in her life. In Romans 14:8-9, God reminds the Christian of that fact in these words:

For none of us liveth to himself, and no man dieth to himself. For whether we live, we live unto the LORD; and whether we die, we die unto the LORD: whether we live therefore, or die, we are the LORD's. For to this end Christ both died, and rose, and revived, that he might be LORD both of the dead and living.

May 18 was a busy day. After work, I went early to Dunkin' Donuts to meet with one of my counselors. (I am habitually early to most meetings.) Sitting in my car in the parking lot, I read the third and fourth chapter of *The Emotionally Destructive Marriage* by Leslie Vernick. Though my thoughts do not correlate perfectly with this helpful book, I wrote the following in my journal:

- Why I sin is part of repentance.
- What I don't give my wife that is loving matters along with what I do that is abusive.
- More revelations of my selfishness: my sin was about me and my wants.
- I have been generous with others and selfish at home.
- Suzanne does not belong to me; she belongs to God and is my partner.
- --Insecure Pride--

- Entitlement: page 94
- Competition; for example, we always played my kind of games
- Envy (page 96) as Saul envied David

The one thought about competition birthed a big and symbolic move. As a couple and as a family, we played many games, but I had adamantly refused to play anything that had to do with luck. Cards, dice, and spinners were all taboo. To play in our house, one had to play games of strategy or word games. Of course, those were my fortes, and I always won.

Allow me to leave the parking lot of Dunkin' Donuts for a few paragraphs to talk about a game and its misadventures in May. I will return momentarily to meet with my mentor, Pastor Bob.

In thirty years of marriage, Suzanne may have beaten me four or five times at a table game of any kind. I have always said of one game, though, that Suzanne could whip me mercilessly any day of the week and twice on Sunday. That game is Ping Pong™. In my best ghetto voice, I would say, "Sister got skills!"

Our house has less than 1400-square feet. We had a larger-than-average kitchen and a piano, but no room for a game that required people to stand on opposite ends of a nine-foot-long table…or was there?

I had already moved the piano, so next I disassembled the La-Z-Boy couch and moved it to the piano room. I added the television, its stand, and the La-Z-Boy recliner. With these changes and additions, the piano room became a nook. I then moved Suzanne's office from the backroom to the place where the television had been. Filing cabinets, junk drawer, and storage cabinets were all moved. Voilà! We now had room for a Ping Pong™ table—with only one problem.

The table would have to be set up in front of the picture window that showed our backyard, which is nearly as long as a football field. Suzanne loved that view. How could I put a big green table in front of it? Mine might be a nice sentiment, but I knew my doing so would annoy her royally.

I knew that folding Ping Pong™ tables can be moved to the side, and I also knew that's the kind she would love. However, that huge green table would completely cover one wall of the room that occupies a third of our tiny house. Necessity is the mother of invention, and though what I did next is really beyond my skill set, I designed a divider that would hide the Ping Pong™ table. This masterpiece of my mind would be the same color as the walls, would be covered with family pictures, and would be an exact fit to hide a big, ugly table! Suzanne had long wanted a way to display a lot of family pictures.

I started building my divider and shopping for a table the next day. That was one of those fun moments. I found myself on the back porch sawing, drilling, and driving screws into my new creation. I was full of energy as I built the piece of furniture that would symbolize a move from my preferences to hers. My building prowess was proving quite suitable for the task at hand until I missed the board with the drill and drilled a hole in my thumb.

Blood was flowing, and I was alone. A longtime habit of mine has been to completely come unglued at the sight of my own blood. I can easily care for a person needing first aid, and I can soak up as much of someone else's blood as is needed, but in this case, I was staring at MY blood. I literally told myself out loud, "You cannot pass out!"

Spoiler alert: I survived! The construction project was stalled for about thirty minutes. As soon as I had the blood stopped, I was back at it. Eventually I had a six-foot-tall rolling divider with ten giant Plexiglas picture frames filled with pictures. I painted the divider the same color as the walls, and I added a drape at the bottom made of the same material as the drapes in the room. My symbol of change was underway.

As I continued to deal with my thumb, I began to wonder about the future. Suzanne had a protection order in place, and on May 26, it would become permanent. Once that happened, she could not drop it at any time. She would have to go to court and explain such a decision to a judge. This exercise would take weeks. Neither she nor anyone else could give me permission to breach the order. What if one of us were injured or truly ill? Would she come to me? Could a lawyer get permission for me to go her?

Uncertainty is a frequent ghost in the haunted house of isolation, casting shadows of imagination on the walls of a lonely mind. Spiritual warfare is fought in such places. When such thoughts invade the mind, one instinctively knows that they are out of place, but what is the person entertaining them to do? The battle of the imagination was one that would be fought in endless skirmishes for many weeks. This ground in my spiritual war would not be won until August, and my own sin of exalting my mind above the knowledge of God would inflict wounds in my soul on a nearly daily basis.

Sins of imagination are some of Satan's most effective fiery darts, and he relentlessly lobs them over the walls of conscious thought. The mind of man is the gateway to his heart, and this heart must be kept with all diligence, for out of it are the issues of life (Proverbs 4:23).

Without further ado, I return to the parking lot of Dunkin' Donuts where I saw Pastor Bob park a few spaces away from my car. Bob possesses a God-given gift for making practical sense of the Bible, which was one reason why I was so glad that he was willing to share his time with me. After meeting with Bob, I made the following notes:

- Bob respects Cyndilu as an equal.
- Bob always works on himself; when issues arise, it is his position, as husband, to be better.
- You cannot promise perfection.
- Bob believes in orders of protection for cases of abuse.
- (Read books by the author) Jay Adams on Marriage
- (I ordered the book.)
- My insecurity is demanding.
- I Peter 2 and 3 teaches the following:
- Be aware of her needs.
- Words are the most damning thing we can do.
- "According to knowledge"—know her temperament and what hurts and helps her.
- "She's my wife; not my daughter."
- Honor my wife; value what she thinks.
- Give her an amount equal to what I spend on myself.
- When an argument means someone wins, it means someone loses, and that's wrong.

At 7:30 that night I met with Paul, a man who has his own story of miraculous grace to tell. My life was 100 percent about becoming who God needed me to be so that Suzanne could be free to come home. For thirteen days I had breathed, eaten, and slept repentance and recovery, but my grief was still very heavy. The biggest burden I listed in my journal was the desire to express love to Suzanne. Knowing I could not so much as ask Paul to give her my love and greatly yearning to do so, I went back to working on the house. I consoled myself in the thought that while I could not express my love with words, I could do so with my hands.

Exercise and diet are often mentioned in the same breath. I improved in both areas, but for very different reasons. The beans and quinoa diet was an attempt to have a clean soul for prayer. Exercise was a way to have a clean mind. Both were attempts to reduce my weight to address my chronic pain condition. I walked and jogged three to five miles per day. With godly, uplifting music in my ears and counting steps between walking and jogging, my mind had no room for loneliness, grief, or imaginations. Physical exercise, mental rest, and physical activity in renovating the house became my quiet time.

HOPEFUL HELPS

- The abused need advocates.
- The abused have a right to seek protection from the government.
- The abused have a right to seek protection and help from the church.
- The government and the church and family have responsibilities to protect and aid the abused.
- Exercise.
- Beware of pride.

Settling Down

After work on May 19, I went to the Bible thrift store in Highland to purchase a suitcase for the "personal items" Suzanne had detailed in her protection order that I was not to destroy or prevent her from having. That anyone would think of me as trying to keep anything from her was bizarre.

I then went for a haircut and had an emotional reaction to the experience. Suzanne had almost always cut my hair for thirty years, and I did not want another woman to cut my hair, but a haircut was needful. I noted that haircuts were $10 on Thursdays.

Having some time on my hands, I parked near our church's Christian high school and read from Chapter Five of Leslie Vernick's book, *The Emotionally Destructive Relationship*. I confirmed once again to myself that pride was the root of my sin; I had been idolatrously usurping God in my home. Constant introspection dovetailed into a persistent search for answers.

The day was cold, dark, and drizzly. My mood matched the weather to a "T." Nearly three weeks had passed since Suzanne had left, and I still struggled greatly with the fact that my wife had literally moved out. She had not left for a while; she had moved. I wrote in my journal that "I must operate with grace and trust God."

On my way to dinner, I went by Mark and Missy's house, hoping to get Suzanne's passport for my coming trip to Maine. For some legal matters, I knew that two positive IDs are better than one. The guns that Suzanne had removed were at Mark and Missy's house, and we had always kept the passports locked in the gun safe. Her passport was not in the gun safe, and surprisingly, neither was mine. Suzanne had apparently taken the passports, but I could not figure out why she would take mine. Did Suzanne think I would flee the country? More drizzle.

Not long before, John and Jen had testified to the church about how God had reconciled them after an anger problem. John was one of the first people to approach me after my confession before the church, and I had been invited to his home for dinner.

Although I felt extremely awkward, it was a fantastic treat to eat real food. Jen had prepared a deep-dish lasagna that could win awards. She also had salads and desserts. I ate like a pig. I was embarrassed, but happily so.

After dinner the three of us went into their family room, where both John and Jen walked me through their struggle. The greatest encouragement came in hearing John's testimony. He went through the same exact pattern as I after his wife had left. He turned to God in almost the same exact way and timing as had I, and his change was permanent. My heart was yearning for permanent change. Their separation was only a matter of days, but otherwise their story was very similar. John and Jen recommended three books: *The Power of a Praying Husband*, *Choosing Forgiveness: Your Journey to Freedom*, and *We Wrestle Not*.

May 20 was a mild, partly cloudy Saturday, and after walking with God, I took in some early morning air by walking several miles. I then puttered around the house doing laundry before leaving for yet another meeting with my pastor. As always, he offered gentle guidance and hope.

From my meeting with the pastor, we both went to our church's monthly "Super Saturday Soul-winning" meeting. Jon, a long time deacon and Sunday school teacher, approached me and asked if I could make a couple of visits with him and grab a bite to eat. He and I never did make those visits, but he did give me a couple of hours at Jedi's Garden. Both Pastor Wilkerson and Jon are edifiers. Am I? Are you?

God makes quite a point about the Christian's job in the work of edification. For example, Ephesians 4:11-16, 29 talks about the purpose a child of God has in the church.

...And he gave some, apostles; and some, prophets; and some, evangelists; and some, pastors and teachers; **for the perfecting of the saints***, for the work of the ministry,* **for the edifying of the body of Christ***: till we all come in the unity of the faith, and of the knowledge of the Son of God, unto a perfect man, unto the measure of the stature of the fullness of Christ: that we henceforth be no more children, tossed to and fro, and carried about with every wind of doctrine, by the sleight of men, and cunning craftiness, whereby they lie in wait to deceive; but speaking the truth in love, may grow up into him in all things, which is the head, even Christ: from whom the whole body fitly joined together and compacted by that which every joint supplieth, according to the effectual working in the measure of every part,* **maketh increase of the body unto the edifying of itself in love***.*

Let no corrupt communication proceed out of your mouth, but **that which is good to the use of edifying***, that it may minister grace unto the* *hearers.*

I Corinthians 14, II Corinthians 12, and much of I Timothy, James, and I Peter all speak to the need that people like me have for people like the godly edifiers at First Baptist. A man like me cannot come from decades of doing damage and find his way to love and respect alone. Addicts cannot find their way from decades of addiction and street life to sanctification alone. Brothers and sisters need each other. Somebody needs you.

Late through the night of May 20 and into the wee hours of May 21, I sought for more edification. I searched the Internet looking for conflict resolution or anger management support groups in my area; I found none but those proctored by paid psychotherapists. One can only pay $180/hour for so long.

Off in the distant recesses of my troubled mind, I began to wonder if the day would come when I could go from being part of the problem to becoming part of the solution. I journaled this question: "Is there room for people like young Jon (a man with a somewhat similar story) and me to bring others on this journey?" In II Corinthians 1:4, the Bible tells us that the Father *...comforteth us in all our tribulation, that we may be able to comfort them which are in any trouble, by the comfort wherewith we ourselves are comforted of God.* God was, indeed, comforting me, and He was using gentle, godly Christians to do much of that work.

The edifying continued on Sunday. Dave, the assistant director at Reformers Unanimous in Hammond, invited me to lunch, and a few minutes later, Jeremiah and Ruth made a similar offer. Had I not humbled myself before the church, would I have received such support? Would anyone have known I had a need? I cannot tell, but I do know that the love of God's people was lifting me above the pit of my transgression and guiding me to a future I could not yet comprehend. The help was needed as the path was still dark. I journaled, "My sin is a runaway freight train. Though I have killed the engine of my sin, 30 years of carnal freight is plowing forward, wreaking havoc and destruction."

Though I had wistfully wondered if I might someday help others, someday was too far away. Man was not made to receive without giving. If my estranged wife were ever to come home, she needed to find a man with a heart for God pouring into the lives of others. If you've plowed through this book so far, you might guess that I like to write. On the twenty-first, Pastor Keith, the Sunday school superintendent at my church, asked me to write some lessons for the 2017 Vacation Bible School. I wrote one-page lessons on Jesus' healing the blind man, Nicodemus, and the Good Samaritan. Anyone could have done the work on these short lessons, but the church gave me the opportunity, and I loved it. I also started baking treats for Sunday school.

Days trudged forward at an agonizingly slow pace. The respites came as people afforded me time. Nearly every evening I had a prayer time with Bob Weer. Wayne began meeting me at Planet Fitness for exercise. My four counselors were part of the cadence, and as regimented as my life was, it was also tormented.

With the court order in place, I could not so much as answer the phone if Suzanne happened to call. I longed to know what she was thinking, but the deafening silence persisted and was joined by the increasingly aggressive insistence from her brother that I should not go to Maine for the hearing. That thought was out of the question; I KNEW that I had to see her. I was sure that if she saw me, she would be able to tell that a difference had been made and that the sight of me would tug at her heartstrings. I also knew that if there were any adverse motions in court, my best place to be was there with my lawyer.

On the twenty-second, I struggled between my great loneliness and the realization that I was not yet ready to be the husband Suzanne needed. I knew that she must be suffering still, and my grief was mingled with guilt. I spoke with my son and with Suzanne's best friend, Missy.

I began to collect letters of commendation for the court hearing. My counselor's letters were the ones I wanted most. I believed that not only would their views be important to the judge but also to Suzanne. Everyone was on board, and I had my letters. The last one that I would collect would be from Steve, my therapist.

On May 23, I met with Steve. We talked about the trip to Maine, and he withdrew his letter. My motives, by Steve's reckoning, were wrong. Going to Maine to have an impact on Suzanne was manipulative. I was, according to him, determining for her what she needed and deciding to give it to her. My brother-in-law had warned me about his belief that Suzanne could have a post-traumatic-stress reaction to seeing me, and Steve reminded me that she had a protection order in place, forbidding me to contact her.

My brother-in-law's assertion of Suzanne's having a PTSD response to seeing me was not at all farfetched to Steve. I was confused. My wife's letter had not indicated that she was afraid of me, but she had said nothing to me at all in nearly three weeks. Nobody was speaking to me on her behalf, and for me to ask anyone to speak to her on my behalf was illegal. How was I to know? What was I to do?

What would it be like to be Suzanne? Could it be true that she was terrified of me? Since she had all this time without me to remember the previous thirty years, I began to wonder what memories she would face. Those outlined in the protection order were awful. Would her memories come back in force? Would they haunt her? Was she tortured? That was not how the wife I knew lived, but then again, I had never really thought of her as being one to leave me.

Numerous studies have been conducted on post-traumatic stress in victims of domestic abuse. The subjects vary greatly, and most are written for the medical community, but they seem to indicate that somewhere between nineteen and thirty-seven percent of women who have suffered abuse are prone to PTSD. I realize the percentage spread is huge, but the short story is that a PTSD response could not be considered "out of the question."

I faced a couple of facts. **First, whether or not Suzanne ever returned, I could not be the same selfish and self-serving person.** Second, **something had to change on the inside**, and the words that came to my mind were "First, do no harm." Just that quickly, the matter was settled in my mind; I could not risk going to Maine. If there was any real chance that my presence would cause a PTSD type of reaction, then I could not do that to my wife.

My heart was crushed. I drove by the house from Steve's office to pick up the necessary items and then drove straight to UPS to overnight the items my lawyer would need for court. I sent Suzanne's birth certificate, her social security card, her cell phone, and a certified check for what I thought was a monumental amount of money. Even if she could not see my face, I wanted her to see as much of my heart as possible. I wanted her to know I was supporting her efforts to get help and to find healing. I longed to show Suzanne love, but the law was very clear, and through the court order, so was the will of my wife. I could do nothing to communicate my heart to Suzanne.

Thankfully again, Wayne took me for a workout after work. Later at church, I explained to the pastor why I had abandoned my trip to Maine. Such decisions can be hard, but if I were to truly repent, I had to find ways to put Suzanne's needs and desires above my own.

As the court date approached, I was hopeful. So many people had told me that Suzanne could change the court order at any time. This date was her last chance, and Becky, my lawyer, was ready to make several good offers and requests.

I was ready to offer financial support, so I asked Becky to add $100 per paycheck to any request Suzanne made up to the point where I thought I could not afford to pay my bills. I was asking for modifications to the order that would allow Suzanne to initiate contact, which would leave all of the power in her hands. If she called, I could answer; if she emailed, I could respond with one non-threatening message; if she were to text me, I could respond with one non-threatening message. Becky agreed that mine were all more-than-reasonable requests. I was certain that we were on the road to reconciliation. In fact, I was so sure that I went out and bought the ingredients for a "feast with Jesus" to celebrate the victory. The closer the moment came, the higher my hopes rose and the more jubilant my spirit soared in anticipation of the beginning of the end. Soon I would say, "It was not to be."

HOPEFUL HELPS

- Sin has consequences.
- Humility attracts helpers.
- We, the church, must edify each other.
- Beware of pride.

Settling In

I rose without an alarm and began praying at 3:00 a.m. Bob Weer arrived early, and we prayed together for 15 minutes. When the phone rang my lawyer began to explain the situation. I went completely numb.

Suzanne did not have the widely regarded expert lawyer I had been told she would have. She had a student lawyer. I was told that Suzanne had completely refused to speak with my attorney. Her monetary demands were for more than half of my take-home pay. She had jotted down a handwritten budget, and from my vantage point, she was asking for:

- Nearly as much grocery money as the two of us had budgeted
- More money for clothes than she had ever spent
- More money for gas than we had budgeted for the two of us
- A very specific amount for a car payment
- Rent and utilities, which signaled to me that she would lease a house or an apartment for a permanent residence
- Enough money for dog care to groom the dog with every paycheck and have enough money left each month to feed him for a year.

She rejected every one of my requests. As the day unfolded, Bob and I were dumbfounded with each new development. There had been no communication with my lawyer, and in so many ways, the day looked bleak. I realized the breakthrough I had anticipated was simply not to be. In fact, as the dust began to settle, Bob and I both believed that the marriage was over. To Bob and to me, this news looked like the opening salvo in an ugly divorce assault.

I knew that I did not deserve to have my wife return. I knew that the issues at hand were both real and serious. Even so, I had read and re-read her "Dear John" letter countless times and felt that she had left behind a note of promise and reconciliation. I knew the letter had been written with a lot of toughness and a lot of love. She had even begun with the words, "Dear Sweetheart, I LOVE YOU! Without a shadow of a doubt I love you and am glad to be your wife. I want to be your wife. I love being your wife…" Now those words rang hollow in my mind.

My kindnesses in sending Suzanne items she had not actually requested, along with a very large check, did not seem to be recognized as kindnesses at all. The strategy of offering Suzanne more support than she had sought never came to fruition, as I was not sure how to pay my bills with the requirements as they were.

As it became evident how the day would end, Bob left, leaving me alone with my thoughts. The situation turned worse yet again, and eventually we knew what the terms would be. I received a final call from Becky, and in following her advice, I began to protect myself financially. I had previously changed all of the passwords to all financial logins, but now I took away Suzanne's access to all of the credit cards. Somewhere in the night, I fell asleep.

The next day I journaled the following:

Court was worse than I ever could have imagined. I had such high hopes for progress, but it was not to be. Suzanne's actions were angry, vengeful, and hateful. I had prepared for a celebratory "feast with Jesus." As the day began and as Becky made me aware of Suzanne's positions, I went numb. I felt nothing. Bob Weer, who was with me, and I both became convinced that the marriage was over.

Suzanne's words say reconciliation, but her actions say vengeful divorce. I have begun the process of defending myself financially. After the mortgage is paid, I will close the current Chase accounts and start new ones. I have removed Suzanne from all credit cards.

Today the emotion came back. I am devastated, but I am committed to continue becoming the man she deserves. Hope has all but perished. I am anguished.

I did walk with the LORD this morning, but I did not record my thoughts here. My future is a black hole. I cannot and will not imagine life without Suzanne, but I see the end. Hope is dying.

As I consider the crushing blow of May 26, I am reminded of the story of "A Traitor Meeting His King."

A brash young soldier had been bribed with fool's gold and had sold out the armies of his lord. He had donned the armor of the enemy and had crawled through the muck of a stagnant pond with poison in his hand. He had brought death into the camp of a pivotal battle to poison the troops of his native country when he was caught red-handed.

Worthy of death, the lad was brought before the king on the outskirts of the battle. The wise ruler was presented with the bag of fool's gold, the vial of poison, and the shamed deserter still wearing the enemy's armor. Strong soldiers stood by, swords drawn, ready to execute the lad. As he beheld the foolish youth, the king gave his sentence.

"Clean up the boy. Feed him well, and give him a good, comfortable night's sleep in the company of my officers. Scrub that ridiculous coat of mail so that it can withstand battle, and put him back into my service. I am adopting him as my son, and when this battle is over, I will replace that bag of fool's gold with treasure. At day's end, he shall become a prince."

Astonished, the lad fell to his knees and wept. He tried to express his sorrow for his deeds, his joy at his fortune, and his love for the generous lord, but words failed him. Only sobs came forth. The king reached down and stood the boy to his feet. He hugged the lad and told him to face the battle with courage. Then he ordered two of his valiant, mighty men to flank the boy into battle to make sure he would survive victoriously.

Presently, the king's men brought forward a bruised and bloodied girl. Beside her stood the husband of her youth who had savagely beaten her, tortured her, and murdered their child. The king drew his own sword beheading the deplorable husband on the spot. He called quickly for his handmaids and told them to wash, feed, and bandage the girl.

On the battlefield, the king had no robes fitting for the occasion, but on the spot he married the girl and told her she would be his true love. Still clothed in her rags, he gave her a tent and told her to wait for the close of the day when he would bring her with him to live out her days in splendor.

For the remainder of the battle, he gave his new bride care over the nursery of his own children and assigned a band of warriors to protect her until the battle's end. She, like the traitor, could not believe what was done for her. She fell on her face and wept tears of joy.

Both the king's new heir and his new bride were still clothed in the rags of their wretched lives, but they were assured of the king's love as the day of battle pressed on and as victory drew near. By nightfall of the next day, both would be in the palace as royalty.

Of course, the king in the allegory is the King of kings. The traitor and the bride are two representations of God's children. The mighty men flanking the traitor are Goodness and Mercy. Consider God's admonition in Romans 6:12-22, and look for yourself at the delivered traitor still wearing the armor of the enemy but destined to rule with the King:

Let not sin therefore reign in your mortal body, that ye should obey it in the lusts thereof. Neither yield ye your members as instruments of unrighteousness unto sin: but yield yourselves unto God, as those that are alive from the dead, and your members as instruments of righteousness unto God. For sin shall not have dominion over you: for ye are not under the law, but under grace.

What then? shall we sin, because we are not under the law, but under grace? God forbid. Know ye not, that to whom ye yield yourselves servants to obey, his servants ye are to whom ye obey; whether of sin unto death, or of obedience unto righteousness? But God be thanked, that ye were the servants of sin, but ye have obeyed from the heart that form of doctrine which was delivered you. Being then made free from sin, ye became the servants of righteousness. I speak after the manner of men because of the infirmity of your flesh: for as ye have yielded your members servants to uncleanness and to iniquity unto iniquity; even so now yield your members servants to righteousness unto holiness. For when ye were the servants of sin, ye were free from righteousness. What fruit had ye then in those things whereof ye are now ashamed? for the end of those things is death. But now being made free from sin, and become servants to God, ye have your fruit unto holiness, and the end everlasting life.

Continue on assuming the mindset of the bride, reading Romans 7:1-6.

Know ye not, brethren, (for I speak to them that know the law,) how that the law hath dominion over a man as long as he liveth? For the woman which hath an husband is bound by the law to her husband so long as he liveth; but if the husband be dead, she is loosed from the law of her husband. So then if, while her husband liveth, she be married to another man, she shall be called an adulteress: but if her husband be dead, she is free from that law; so that she is no adulteress, though she be married to another man. Wherefore, my brethren, ye also are become dead to the law by the body of Christ; that ye should be married to another, even to him who is raised from the dead, that we should bring forth fruit unto God. For when we were in the flesh, the motions of sins, which were by the law, did work in our members to bring forth fruit unto death. But now we are delivered from the law, that being dead wherein we were held; that we should serve in newness of spirit, and not in the oldness of the letter.

Reading from the vantage of both the traitor and the chosen bride, read these selections of Romans 8, starting with verses 12-21, knowing that our present trials are not fit to be compared to what awaits at His castle:

Therefore, brethren, we are debtors, not to the flesh, to live after the flesh. For if ye live after the flesh, ye shall die: but if ye through the Spirit do mortify the deeds of the body, ye shall live. For as many as are led by the Spirit of God, they are the sons of God. For ye have not received the spirit of bondage again to fear; but ye have received the Spirit of adoption, whereby we cry, Abba, Father. The Spirit itself beareth witness with our spirit, that we are the children of God: and if children, then heirs; heirs of

God, and joint-heirs with Christ; if so be that we suffer with him, that we may be also glorified together.

For I reckon that the sufferings of this present time are not worthy to be compared with the glory which shall be revealed in us. For the earnest expectation of the creature waiteth for the manifestation of the sons of God. For the creature was made subject to vanity, not willingly, but by reason of him who hath subjected the same in hope, because the creature itself also shall be delivered from the bondage of corruption into the glorious liberty of the children of God (continuing in verses 37-39) *in all these things we are more than conquerors through him that loved us. For I am persuaded, that neither death, nor life, nor angels, nor principalities, nor powers, nor things present, nor things to come, nor height, nor depth, nor any other creature, shall be able to separate us from the love of God, which is in Christ Jesus our LORD.*

Does any man stand before the King worthy of death? I do. Was ever a man delivered from the ravages of his own poor choices to have the promise of eternal blessing? I was. Does anyone deserve grace less or receive it more freely than I? No, of course not! Has anyone been blessed with continual goodness and mercy for no apparent reason? It is I. In every way, the allegory is my story, and Romans 6-8 is my promise.

One night in October of 1975, my mother and stepfather had a terrible fight. They screamed, hollered, and threatened each other all night long. Doors slammed, things broke, and Hell itself seemed to invade.

Sometime in the night, I crept into my closet to hide from the brutal conflict. I sat in the darkness, gripping my baseball bat and listening to the waxing and waning of my parents' fury. Shortly before sunrise, the house became quiet. The closet door opened, and my mother stood in front of me. She tossed two paper grocery sacks on the bed. She told me to pack clothes for two weeks in the sack and to go get in the station wagon. My sister and I both did so. I was first, so I had the "shotgun" seat.

After what seemed like forever, Mom brought my baby brother to the car in his car seat and strapped him in. She loaded some belongings into the car and backed out of the driveway. As the sun rose over Austin, Texas, we drove out of the city. I have never been back.

The next summer we were living in El Paso, where mother had begun taking us to a church in town. Attending summer camp with that church family became a pivotal time in my life. The camp we attended was at Sivell's Baptist Camp near Cloudcroft, New Mexico.

On Monday afternoon at camp, we met near a flagpole and began to memorize the week's' verse, Ephesians 2:8. *For by grace are ye saved through faith; and that not of yourselves: it is the gift of God.* We quoted that verse repeatedly all week, and the speaker spoke from it several times.

The speaker was a converted Jew, and I believe his name was Sammy Oppenheim. I have never seen nor heard of him again. He did explain Ephesians 2:8 to the campers that week. Because of his teaching, I accepted that "gift of God." For forty-eight years, even through the thick mess of my abusive behaviors, this "gift of God" has been the central and saving grace of my life. All of the redemptive power that came to me in the summer of 2017 was birthed in America's bicentennial summer in the mountains of New Mexico.

This grace is central to all that God has done for me since Suzanne had the courage to confront my anger and to leave.

Perhaps the most doctrinal book in the New Testament is Romans. It clearly explains the Gospel or the good news of Jesus Christ. The good news starts with a rather bad reality. As an eternal being, I am unfit to live with an eternal God. Romans 3:10 states: *As it is written, There is none righteous, no, not one.*

God emphasizes that "no, not one" person is righteous, though a man such as I can look in the mirror and see that truth clearly. The word *righteous* is not one frequently used in America today, but the root word of *righteous* is *right*. If I were righteous, everything I said would be right; everything I did would be right, and all that I was would be right. If I were righteous, I would be packed full of right, but I am not. If one continues reading through the chapter, she would come to Verse 23, which further explains that: *all have sinned, and come short of the glory of God.*

Sin is breaking God's law. All have broken it and have fallen short. Many Christians use the Ten Commandments as a starting point, and that is a good idea. When the religious people of His day asked Christ which of the Ten Commandments was the greatest, He answered with these words: *Thou shalt love the LORD thy God with all thy heart, and with all thy soul, and with all thy mind. This is the first and great commandment. And the second is like unto it, Thou shalt love thy neighbour as thyself. On these two commandments hang all the law and the prophets.*

If I were to measure myself against those two simple commandments and if I were to use this week as a sample, I fall pitifully short. Loving God with ALL of my heart, soul, and mind? ALL? It has never happened. Loving my neighbor as myself—every neighbor? Always? I have not. In the parable of the Good Samaritan, Jesus describes my neighbor as a member of a different race, a different religion, and a different culture as the example of my neighbor. If loving such a one as I love myself and if loving God with all is the basis for all of God's law, I am in trouble.

The Gospel or good news turns good at this point. If one continues reading through the book of Romans, he will come to Chapter 5 where God explains: *For when we were yet without strength, in due time Christ died for the ungodly. For scarcely for a righteous man will one die: yet peradventure for a good man some would even dare to die. But God commendeth his love toward us, in that, while we were yet sinners, Christ died for us.*

We call that the "vicarious death." Jesus died in my place; the Eternal God died for a mortal man. While I was yet a sinner, Christ died for me. He had to because Romans 6 plainly tells me: ...*the wages of sin is death; but the gift of God is eternal life through Jesus Christ our LORD.*

Day after day, week after week, and year after year I have earned the wages of my sin. In the eternity of an eternal God Who knows every thought and intent of my heart, I fall immeasurably short. Not only do I have sins against me, but I also have no righteousness with which to merit eternal Heaven with God.

Jesus Christ not only paid for every sin I have ever committed and for every sin I will ever commit; He gave me His righteousness as my own. This same Apostle Paul would admonish the church at Corinth in II Corinthians 5:21 with these words: be *ye reconciled to God. For he hath made him to be sin for us, who knew no sin; that we might be made the righteousness of God in him.* (II Corinthians 5:21)

That is my hope. To have righteousness, I needed to have it given to me. To deal with my sin, I needed Someone eternal Who could handle the consequences of my life and my choices. In the courtroom of Heaven, I am justified before the King of all the ages, not because I have righteousness of my own, but because He paid the price for me and gave me that gift of God which is eternal life through Jesus Christ, my LORD.

How does one receive such a gift? The apostle answers that question in Romans 10:8-13:

But what saith it? The word is nigh thee, even in thy mouth, and in thy heart: that is, the word of faith, which we preach; that if thou shalt confess with thy mouth the LORD *Jesus, and shalt believe in thine heart that God hath raised him from the dead, thou shalt be saved. For with the heart man believeth unto righteousness; and with the mouth confession is made unto salvation. For the scripture saith, Whosoever believeth on him shall not be ashamed. For there is no difference between the Jew and the Greek: for the same* LORD *over all is rich unto all that call upon him. For whosoever shall call upon the name of the* LORD *shall be saved.*

Any person who will acknowledge to God that he is guilty of sin and lacking in righteousness can call out to Him for the gift of God, eternal life, believing from the heart and confessing with the mouth the LORD Jesus Christ. If one were to make such a decision, her heart's cry to God might be something like this:

"LORD Jesus, I know I have sinned. I know I do not and cannot deserve eternal life in Heaven, but You can and You do. I believe that You loved me enough to sacrifice Yourself as the payment for my sin and that You willingly offered Your righteous life in the place of my sinful life. May I please accept your offer of eternal life? I accept You as the complete payment for my sin and as all of the righteousness I will ever need."

Though I deserved to be rejected by my bride and though I had betrayed the grace that had saved my soul, I knew on May 27 that the goodness and mercy of Psalm 23 could still follow me all the days of my life and that I could dwell in the house of the LORD forever. I also knew that whether or not Suzanne ever came back, I had to turn to this God who had loved me so unselfishly for mercy and grace. I had to change, and if my soul could be saved from Hell, that same God could give me what I needed for a new life.

Without the gift of God's salvation, I would not have the Holy Spirit living inside of me, and the graces of Romans Chapters 6 through 8 could never be mine.

HOPEFUL HELPS

- Redemption is God's plan.
- Redemption begins with faith in Christ.
- Beware of pride.

Setting Up

Though Sundays were hard days, one in particular helped me begin to come around. I journaled the following:

"...I have Christ" My little children, these things write I unto you, that ye sin not. And if any man sin, we have an advocate with the Father, Jesus Christ the righteous: and he is the propitiation for our sins: and not for ours only, but also for the sins of the whole world. (I John 2:1-2)

AM Service: Ephesians 2:8-10; PM Service: Hebrews II. Both: God is a rewarder. Sundays are emotional days. It's hard to see the choir where Suzanne is not sitting in her usual place, and singing groups that she is not in, etc. It's hard to go to Sunday school and church without her. My heart longs to tell her I love her. I know we are in a long process.

If Suzanne and I were to be reunited, it would clearly be a long process, and several changes would still have to take place in me. I was reading constantly, and I was struggling with how Christian authors wrote about marital abuse and abusers. The descriptions of what real repentance looked like seemed unattainable. The descriptions of what fake repentance looked like seemed to describe me, at least in part.

I knew then, and I know now, that I had truly repented of my symptomatic sins of abuse and my root sin of pride fully on May 5 & 6. My heart had truly cried out to God. I know that He heard me and that my fellowship with Him was restored. I was indeed a different man, but different from abusive does not mean ready to help heal. Humility alone is not enough to change patterns of behavior.

May 29, Memorial Day, was another pivotal point in my journey to a changed life. My "local" kids had invited me over for a picnic, and it was awesome. (My son and my daughter-in-law are both PHENOMENAL cooks!) Before leaving to visit them, I found myself trolling the web, looking for a way to contact Chris Moles. I had been wanting to email him to ask a few questions when I happened upon his page: chrismoles.org. There I read that Chris offered personal coaching to abusive men. Instantly I applied. His book had been so powerful in my life that the idea of learning directly from Chris became an instant passion.

No man can take the place of God. No man can change another, but God uses men to guide men to Himself. The best of men are men at best, and faith in men to do God's work is misplaced faith to be sure. Perhaps I put too much weight on the desire to coach with Chris Moles, but in retrospect, contacting him was the one of best decisions I have ever made.

I recommend Chris Moles. Anyone who has been abusive and wants to learn God's path to a holy life of peace, can learn much from Chris Moles. I hope he continues his ministry, and I pray that God keeps him fit for service. I also hope others rise to join his ranks. He has a training program for churches, and though I do not know the content, I know the author. I also know that the need seems great.

The services Chris provides are not free, and I was in the midst of making significant financial adjustments to meet my court-ordered support obligations. I texted both Mom and Dad, asking if they could help. Both of my parents did help, and though I had not yet been accepted to the program, I knew that I had the financial requirements met.

My time spent with the kids was great. There is nobody like family. The kids also had been in contact with Suzanne and were able to tell me some of what they knew. They believed that the court date had been central in their mom's life and that she had had significant pressure on her up to and through that point.

I helped my son with the grill and tried to be a good dad. I am certain that I must have been awkward, but I could never adequately express how good it was to be loved by my kids. Knowing that Suzanne had the comforts of her family was also good. That night I journaled the following:

Suzanne Marie, I love you with all of my heart. I will never, ever hurt you again. I have plenty of issues to address, and the LORD is addressing them with me, but I will absolutely never hurt you again. This is my vow.

You are going through such an awful time. I should be there to comfort you, to hug you, and to tell you that everything is going to be okay. I am not there because I have sinned against Heaven and in your sight. My privilege to be your friend has been suspended. When we do get to reunite on any level, it will be about you and what you need. This is my promise.

I love you; I love you; I love you; I love you; I love you; I love you; I love you; I love you; I love you; I LOVE YOU!

That night I dreamed in vivid color and with details of a quick, happy reunion. The alarm had been set for 3:30 a.m. I woke before the alarm to the cold, dark, emptiness of the same ugly little dungeon of a bedroom. OUCH! The consequences of thirty years of horrid behavior was an appalling reality.

Even so, I knew that I was not yet ready to be her husband. Emotional conflict is part of the work of transformation. There is never a comfortable move from a lifetime of harm into a ministry of grace. Like any restoration, an abundance of sanding, grinding, banging, and cutting must take place. I believe the work of transformation is reflected in this clip from the journal:

> Suzanne, I love you like I have never loved you. Grace and humility are becoming part of me. Please come home so we can work this out.
>
> I don't really mean home. I would love to have you living nearby so we could date for many weeks. We need to start over where we were 34 years ago...but not take so long this time.
>
> I know you are hurting. I long to help you, comfort you, give you the grace you can get nowhere else."

A journal or diary can be helpful to the writer, and they were to me. As I moved on from the shock of court and the energy that I had put into preparing for it, my life continued to be focused on mending my life with the LORD. Whether married, separated, or divorced, I knew I needed to be different. Though I had repented, I wanted to be someone God could use.

I could not understand it fully at the time, but this point must be stressed. God's work on *me*. For repentance to yield her fruit she must lead a man to Christ. When a man has committed horrible crimes, he must be focused on God—not on reconciliation. This is counterintuitive to man apart from his wife, but it is vitally true.

My thirty years of marriage could be summed up accurately in Matthew 23:23-28: *Woe unto you, scribes and Pharisees, hypocrites! for ye pay tithe of mint and anise and cumin, and have omitted the weightier matters of the law, judgment, mercy, and faith: these ought ye to have done, and not to leave the other undone. Ye blind guides, which strain at a gnat, and swallow a camel. Woe unto you, scribes and Pharisees, hypocrites! for ye make clean the outside of the cup and of the platter, but within they are full of extortion and excess. Thou blind Pharisee, cleanse first that which is within the cup and platter, that the outside of them may be clean also. Woe unto you, scribes and Pharisees, hypocrites! for ye are like unto whited sepulchers, which indeed appear beautiful outward, but are within full of dead men's bones, and of all uncleanness. Even so ye also outwardly appear righteous unto men, but within ye are full of hypocrisy and iniquity.*

No group gave the Saviour heartburn quite like the Pharisees. I, like they, had focused much of my life on appearance. I did, indeed, tithe religiously but likewise passed over judgment, mercy, and faith. If I was ever to be fit to lead a family, faith would need to lead me to mercy and judgment.

Distinguishing between righteous acts and self-righteous acts is tricky business, but perhaps faith is the key. Christianity is to flow from the Spirit dwelling within to minister to those without. It is not meant to be pushed in from a husband or a father or a pastor or any other human from the outside.

Virtually everyone was shocked to know that our home had been a place of abuse. A family or two who had been close to Suzanne knew that she and I had a history, but only those who had lived within our four walls had an inkling of the truth. Appearing righteous while full of hypocrisy had to end in my life, and something truly beautiful had to begin.

Hypocrisy kills in the abusive home, and it kills silently. It wrecks the security of children who are forced to keep the family secret, and it poisons the faith of the wife who cannot call out for help. Victims become actors worthy of Oscars. The façade of life is so real that outsiders *never* know.

On Tuesday morning, life continued as though there had been no holiday. I did not know how long the separation would continue, but this lifestyle was the new normal. I lived to become what God and Suzanne needed me to be. Part of that was work, part of that was study, part of that was counsel, a part was improving my health, but a huge part it was prayer. Steve, my patient therapist, said that it was clear that I was "all-in." If this was to be the Refiner's fire, then I truly wanted the furnace blasting at maximum heat.

Divorce had never been a part of my consciousness, but now it looked like I might be headed there. What if she filed? How does that work? If she files first, will I have to go to court in Maine? These responses were further proof that some necessary work still needed to be done in my heart.

I did learn the process, and I found that Suzanne had to be in Maine for six months to file there and that she had already been out of Indiana for too long to file in Indiana anytime soon. The six-month requirement in Maine meant that she would be eligible to file on November 3, but both states would recognize that the case would have to be decided under Indiana law.

I circled a date on the calendar under the mistaken belief that I would need to file first to protect myself. If the conditions I had in mind were not met by that date, I would file. Part of me knew that the consequences of my actions were less than I deserved, but part of me wanted the best possible outcome if divorce became reality. *A double minded man is unstable in all of his ways.* (James 1:8)

The date on the calendar, which was mostly an escape from the pressure of my solitude, was an imaginary light at the end of some tunnel whereby I could limit the length of my sentence. Filing for divorce could not alleviate any suffering; it could only cause suffering. Such a move would have been a selfish "solution" to a self-inflicted wound. My entire thought process was an attempt to manufacture hope, and the hope of God's children should be in the LORD.

For the sake of healing, Suzanne needed solitude. An abuse victim in unrestricted contact with her tormentor can be likened to a camper alone in the wilderness being circled all night by a wounded animal. The tormentor does nothing to bring comfort or peace. In the quiet of her prayer closet and free from the din of my yammering laments, perhaps Suzanne could find peace with God. That one value alone when filing an order of protection frees the oppressed to focus on matters of eternal importance while letting the oppressor to do the same.

The book *Crazy Love* by Francis Chan was a challenge to a divorce-as-an-escape way of thinking. In fact, the book is a challenge to any carnal or lazy way of thinking. As May gave way to June, I read the book and realized it questioned my concept of what it meant to love God. While reading *Crazy Love*, my Bible time was in the Proverbs, and my counselors were pointing me toward stability. My journal entry for May 30 included the following thoughts:

My sleep is mostly peaceful, but the heartache does cost me sometimes. Last night I dreamed of a quick reunion and woke to find it fantasy. OUCH!

Proverbs 14:17, *He that is soon angry dealeth foolishly.* Proverbs 14:29, *He that is slow to wrath is of great understanding.* Proverbs 15:1, *A soft answer turneth away wrath: but grievous words stir up anger.* Proverbs 16:1, *The preparations of the heart in man, and the answer of the tongue, is from the LORD.*

I closed my June 1 journal entry with these words:

Suzanne, I love you, and I hurt for you. I stole the best years of your life, and now I am reaping the wind. I vow that I will never hurt you again, and I am committed to seeing the changes that God wants to make in me. I pray for you constantly.

My journal entries would continue for some time with notes to Suzanne. The protection order said that she could call me, but the phone did not ring. I had no official word from my wife, but everyone around me seemed convinced that the first call would come on July 2, our thirtieth wedding anniversary. Morning by morning I prayed and sought God; day by day I worked and waited, night by night I prayed again, and I hoped.

Not long after court, Tony, the Director of our Reformers Unanimous program, called and invited me back to my role on Friday nights. My small group had been assigned to another leader, but Tony was planning to start a new group for me. June 2 was my first Friday night back in a ministry. I wept through a testimony, and many of the men responded with encouragement. Some said that my testimony was helpful.

June 6 was a good day. I picked up the phone and called an old friend, Craig. For years Craig and I had visited together for an adult Sunday school class. He had taught me a bit about hunting, and our wives had become fast friends. The truth was that Craig had been the last friend to whom I had been close, and we had been mostly out of touch since he had moved to West Virginia a decade and a half earlier. Craig had been pastoring for several years and had counseled many people through tough situations, but more importantly, he was a real friend in every sense of the word. Pastor Craig KNEW me, and he also knew Suzanne. After a long and painful explanation, he joined the ranks of my counselors. Other than my own pastor, Pastor Wilkerson, nobody would spend as much time working with me in the months to come as Pastor Craig.

Craig listened at length—great length—to my thinking every Saturday morning at 5:00. Often we would be on the phone for as long as two hours. He listened for intent, motive, and reasoning. With gentle frankness, he pointed out the places where my ways were askew from God's ways, but he was always encouraging. God brought him to my side at a perfect time.

HOPEFUL HELPS

- Journal, especially during the transitions of life,
- One fruit of repentance is an "all-in" commitment.
- Seek godly counsel.
- Beware of pride.

Being One

The next day, June 7, my Bible reading brought me across a most interesting account in the tenth chapter of Mark. The mother of James and John had just come to Jesus, asking Him to promote her two boys in His kingdom. The other disciples were quite unhappy, so Jesus called them together. He explained Christian leadership in Mark 10:42-45 with these words: *Ye know that they which are accounted to rule over the Gentiles exercise lordship over them; and their great ones exercise authority upon them. But so shall it not be among you: but whosoever will be great among you, shall be your minister: and whosoever of you will be the chiefest, shall be servant of all. For even the Son of man came not to be ministered unto, but to minister, and to give his life a ransom for many.*

I realized the words, *"But so shall it NOT be among you,"* described exactly what was wrong with my attitude in marriage. If I wanted to learn to love my wife *"even as Christ also loved the church, and gave himself for it,"* then giving my life had to be central. The concepts of being a minister and a servant and of giving my life as a ransom was to be the new paradigm, and what a tall order it was!

To my own Master I stand or fall. The evil I committed was mine alone and not another's with me. No false teaching or poorly worded lesson can be brought with me into judgment when I stand before God, but a serious need for improvement exists in the evangelical world.

Statistically, from the standpoint of faith, the LEAST likely man to commit abuse was an "Active Conservative Protestant." It would be nice for "Conservative Protestants" if that was the end of the matter. Unfortunately, the man MOST likely to commit domestic violence was the "Nominal Conservative Protestant." (Wilcox, 2004) The stark contrasts between the two groups do not end there. They are repeated in areas of understanding, communication, and appreciation. The tie between the pulpit and the pew is vital. Whatever else one may derive from the works of scholars, Mr. Wilcox makes it plain that there is a significant opportunity within the community of a church congregation to affect the likelihood of domestic abuse.

Jason Meyer of the Bethlehem Baptist Church in the Minneapolis area, a man of whom I had never heard, had preached an impactful sermon in

April of 2015. He had delivered the sermon entitled "Fooled by False Leadership." (Meyer, 2015) As of this writing, the entire sermon is still in print on the church's website. In his sermon, Pastor Meyer called out domestic abuse and called on his church to address the matter. In that sermon he uses, and perhaps coins, the term *hyper-headship*. This term describes the way in which I had justified myself in many areas of my sin.

A frequently quoted outtake of that sermon is as follows:

"Hyper-headship is a satanic distortion of male leadership, but it can fly under the radar of discernment because it is disguised as strong male leadership. Make no mistake—it is harsh, oppressive, and controlling. In other words, hyper-headship becomes a breeding ground for domestic abuse."

I had hidden my sin from myself with that very disguise. In like manner, good Bible-believing churches can, in fact, unwittingly become such breeding grounds. Did not Satan attempt to tempt Christ Himself with distortions of the Scriptures? Were not Satan's first recorded words to mankind, *"Yea, hath God said…?"* (Genesis 3:1).

I have never heard a sermon directly say that it is acceptable for a husband to be harsh, oppressive, or controlling to his wife. I have seen what Jason Meyer describes. "Hussy" and "Jezebel" are never proper terms for describing wives or women whose philosophies differ from one's own. Never. Sir or madam, please examine your own teaching. Does it rightly divide the Word of Truth along these lines?

When the roles of marriage are distorted to put insufficient weight on the sacrifice and servitude of a godly husband, temptations toward pride are inevitable. I have heard many godly Bible teachers, including my own pastor, as well as Pastor Bob, properly describe the Biblical roles of marriage, but I have also heard sermons and outtakes from sermons which proliferated the very distortion Jason Meyer called his church to address. Kudos, Pastor Meyer.

In my tightly focused reading after Suzanne left, I learned much of this problem. One of the closest tools to a solution in print may be *The Exemplary Husband* by Stuart Scott. I realize that I have already mentioned the text, but Mr. Scott has done the Christian world a favor by publishing his book.

To contrast the notion of strong, Biblically loving leadership in a home with that pattern of sin Mr. Meyer calls hyper-headship, please consider

Mark 10:42-45 once more.

*Ye know that they which are accounted to rule over the Gentiles exercise lordship **over** them; and their great ones exercise authority **upon** them. But so shall it not be among you: but whosoever will be great among you, shall be your minister: and whosoever of you will be the chiefest, shall be servant of all. For even the Son of man came not to be ministered unto, but to minister, and to give his life a ransom for many.*

The servant of all giving his life for his followers is exactly what strong, Christian leadership looks like. One who leads like Christ can never be mistaken for an ogre. Search the Scriptures for a time when Jesus harshly compelled His followers; it does not exist. A Christian leader seeks not to be ministered to, but to minister and to give. It's a tall order.

When reading books, it is easy to skim over passages of Scripture. All scripture should be delightfully read and carefully considered.

When Paul wrote to the church at Ephesus, he wrote one letter. He did not divide it into chapters and verses. Translators did that for the sake convenience. Early in the letter Paul, through the Holy Ghost, established the Headship of Christ. Consider Ephesians 1:20-22.

Which he wrought in Christ, when he raised him from the dead, and set him at his own right hand in the heavenly places, far above all principality, and power, and might, and dominion, and every name that is named, not only in this world, but also in that which is to come: and hath put all things under his feet, and gave him to be the head over all things to the church, which is his body, the fulness of him that filleth all in all.

In Chapter 3 the goal of love is established in verses 14-19.

For this cause I bow my knees unto the Father of our Lord Jesus Christ, of whom the whole family in heaven and earth is named, that he would grant you, according to the riches of his glory, to be strengthened with might by his Spirit in the inner man; that Christ may dwell in your hearts by faith; that ye, being rooted and grounded in love, may be able to comprehend with all saints what is the breadth, and length, and depth, and height; and to know the love of Christ, which passeth knowledge, that ye might be filled with all the fulness of God.

God shows Christians a bit of what loves acts like in Ephesians 4:29-5:2. *Let no corrupt communication proceed out of your mouth, but that which is good to the use of edifying, that it may minister grace unto the hearers. And grieve not the holy Spirit of God, whereby ye are sealed unto the day of redemption. Let all bitterness, and wrath, and anger, and clamour, and evil speaking, be put away from you, with all malice: and be ye kind one to another, tenderhearted, forgiving one another, even as God for Christ's sake hath forgiven you.*

Be ye therefore followers of God, as dear children; and walk in love, as Christ also hath loved us, and hath given himself for us an offering and a sacrifice to God for a sweetsmelling savour.

One should examine carefully all that comes before and after, along with Ephesians 5:18-33. It is in this context that we are taught of God to see His priorities in relationships. Knowing the Headship of Christ, God's emphasis on love, and His description of love, perhaps one can then read God's priorities for relationships in context.

And be not drunk with wine, wherein is excess; but be filled with the Spirit; speaking to yourselves in psalms and hymns and spiritual songs, singing and making melody in your heart to the Lord; giving thanks always for all things unto God and the Father in the name of our Lord Jesus Christ; submitting yourselves one to another in the fear of God.

Wives, submit yourselves unto your own husbands, as unto the Lord. For the husband is the head of the wife, even as Christ is the head of the church: and he is the saviour of the body. Therefore as the church is subject unto Christ, so let the wives be to their own husbands in every thing. Husbands, love your wives, even as Christ also loved the church, and gave himself for it; that he might sanctify and cleanse it with the washing of water by the word, that he might present it to himself a glorious church, not having spot, or wrinkle, or any such thing; but that it should be holy and without blemish. So ought men to love their wives as their own bodies. He that loveth his wife loveth himself. For no man ever yet hated his own flesh; but nourisheth and cherisheth it, even as the Lord the church: for we are members of his body, of his flesh, and of his bones. For this cause shall a man leave his father and mother, and shall be joined unto his wife, and they two shall be one flesh. This is a great mystery: but I speak concerning Christ and the church. Nevertheless let every one of you in particular so love his wife even as himself; and the wife see that she reverence her husband.

Churches have at least three responsibilities to men who commit sins of domestic abuse. The first task is undoubtedly the most difficult task: prevent domestic abuse. If churches are to make progress in this area, the progress will be on purpose. Leadership will have to acknowledge the problem, recognize its role, and take the message to the men. Thankfully, the matter of premarital counseling provides an opportunity. Many churches have taken steps towards prevention at exactly this spot. One might ask if his church has done so and if such counseling is mandatory.

The second responsibility can be seen in the matter of church discipline as introduced by the LORD Himself in Matthew 18 and as affirmed by the Holy Spirit in I Corinthians 6. Certainly an abused woman has rights before the law and is within Scriptural standing before God to invoke that protection when it is needed. Nevertheless, the church may not excuse itself from the obligation to protect the members of its own family—the family of God.

The third responsibility is to restore those who repent. Christians are to forgive and comfort that they might confirm their love so that Christ and not Satan should have the advantage in the lives of those who have done the worst. Much of my story is the story of my church doing exactly that.

The Apostle Paul dealt with one man's sin in both books of the Corinthians. One particular man was committing adultery with his stepmother. The church was celebrating the fact that they were accepting of such a person. In his first letter to the Corinthian people, the apostle sternly warned the church not to put up with such sin in their congregation, and they obeyed in I Corinthians 5:1-2.

It is reported commonly that there is fornication among you, and such fornication as is not so much as named among the Gentiles, that one should have his father's wife. And ye are puffed up, and have not rather mourned, that he that hath done this deed might be taken away from among you.

The apostle covers the situation at length. A brief but important piece of the conversation is in I Corinthians 5:13.

But them that are without God judgeth. Therefore put away from among yourselves that wicked person.

In his second letter to the church, Paul admonished the Corinthias again that they should receive the man who had fornicated with his stepmother because that man had repented. The apostle explained this in II Corinthians 2:6-11.

Sufficient to such a man is this punishment, which was inflicted of many. So that contrariwise ye ought rather to forgive him, and comfort him, lest perhaps such a one should be swallowed up with overmuch sorrow. Wherefore I beseech you that ye would confirm your love toward

him. For to this end also did I write, that I might know the proof of you,
whether ye be obedient in all things. To whom ye forgive any thing, I
forgive also: for if I forgave any thing, to whom I forgave it, for your sakes
forgave I it in the person of Christ; lest Satan should get an advantage of
us: for we are not ignorant of his devices.

Satan wants to steal, kill, and destroy. As the LORD Himself pointed out
through Micaiah in I Kings 22, the Evil One has few tools as lethal as a
lying spirit in the mouth of a prophet. As one who has inflicted much
damage from a false assertion of pseudo-Biblical authority, may I please
implore those who preach on this topic to address and describe carefully
the role of the servant-leader anytime headship or submission enters the
discussion? Having addressed that issue at length, I return to the narrative.

On June 10, I helped Wayne with an errand that took me to his house.
While I was there, I received a call from Pastor Wilkerson. He wanted to
talk to me about a concern Suzanne had. She wanted my therapist to talk to
her therapist before we had our first conversation. I have no possible way
to express how much I wanted to talk to my wife. I had heard that after our
anniversary conversation, she planned to start a regimen of weekly, ten-
minute phone calls. I assumed that the July 2 phone call would also be ten
minutes. Now I was uncertain as to whether this meant we might speak
sooner or if our calls were in doubt altogether.

I was totally engrossed in the communication and found myself telling
Pastor how I would handle it. Then I became afraid that I was participating
in "indirect communication," which could land me in jail. I completely
panicked, asking him NOT to relay any messages. He agreed and
apologized for starting the conversation with me. He did say that in a
conversation that day with Suzanne, she had told him that she "meant
every word" she had written in her letter.

"Every word"… in my mind, that meant that my counselors would
have to tell her that it was safe to come home. That one person can ever
guarantee the behavior of another person is impossible. Did this
conundrum mean that she would never come home? One-way
communication is always an inexact science, but in stressful situations like
mine, describing it would be difficult at best.

I called Suzanne's brother to ask what I should do. He advised me to
have my attorney work it out. I emailed Becky that night, and on Monday
morning, she advised me that my wife's lawyer had been a student on loan

to a legal aid clinic from a law school. Law-school students can be difficult to find in June. I advised my brother-in-law, and a couple of hours later he texted me a photo of a business card. Now I had a way for Steve to contact Suzanne's therapist. Hope and anticipation were mingled with fear.

Sunday, June 11, was a day of invitations. I was invited to the Wilkersons' for lunch. Then some old friends from the bus ministry asked me if I could join them. When I told them where I was going, they promised that a raincheck would be forthcoming. Val and Maury said they would have me soon as did Dan and Beverly. Obviously a lot of people cared for me and Suzanne and wanted to offer me support.

I was quite nervous to have lunch at the pastor's house, though I cannot explain why. I have never been nervous to spend any amount of time with my pastor, for we had already spent an enormous amount of time together, but I was definitely nervous. Mrs. Wilkerson had prepared a huge spread of food of many kinds. Out-of-town guests, who were in full-time Christian service, as well as most of the Wilkersons' eight children were there. We enjoyed a lively, lovely, warm Sunday dinner.

After dinner, Brother John and I went to his office at the church for a counseling session. He recommended the book, *The Slight Edge* by Jeff Olson, which I ordered that night. We spent more than an hour together working on spiritual issues. He was always encouraging and always challenging. I never knew all the ways in which he was working to be impartial between the two of us. Perhaps few can walk the line that he walked to help us both.

On Monday, June 12, I had an interview with Chris Moles. He asked about my salvation testimony and why I needed coaching. He then explained how some of the program worked. He spent about an hour interviewing me and concluded by letting me know that several men were seeking the two available spots. I told him that if I were not chosen for July, I would like to be at the top of the list for the next opening.

That night I met the chairman of our deacons and his wife at Round the Clock, a local family restaurant, for dinner. Elton described a far different relationship with his wife than the relationship between Suzanne and me. Anger and rage were not the only differences. I could clearly see that they were two distinct individuals who respected each other. We three asked questions, shared stories, and spent a tough but delightful time together. I left wanting to be like them.

Something changed in my perception of my church that night. I had already learned that my pastor was strong to defend women in plights like Suzanne's, but he had only been at the church for a few years. In the back of my mind, part of me believed that the "old-school" members were still in the hyper-headship camp. Not so! Elton does not have one second of patience for my brand of foolishness. He was extremely kind and helpful in my restoration, but he made no pretense of support for a domineering male in a home.

Elton was the man to whom the job of forming a discipline committee would have fallen if Suzanne had pursued relief through our church. The church is steadfast and unmovable in its support for the victim. My false doctrines may have been seeded in similar places, but THIS church would have none of it. Everyone has marriage issues, but abuse is not a marital issue. Abuse has a victim, and victims need protectors.

HOPEFUL HELPS

- All authority begins and ends with God.
- Roles in marriage are loving, serving roles.
- Churches have vital roles and responsibilities.
- One must be faithful to the truth, even at the expense of tradition.
- Redemption is God's plan, and He wants to redeem even the vilest.
- The child of God should seek help in the church.
- The church must help the child of God.
- Beware of pride.

Being Blessed

On Sunday morning, June 18, I rose early enough to pray and then walk beneath the summer stars. Sunrise came at 5:18 and found me on my way home from a delightful walk. It was Father's Day. I was alone—alone but at peace. My life was still an emotional and spiritual struggle, but Sundays were becoming my best days. Because it was Father's Day and because my church always has fathers stand to receive a gift, I texted the Weers and told them I would be sitting in the back.

While puttering around the house preparing for Sunday school, I received a Facebook message from my mother-in-law that read: "I know you cannot contact me back, but I just wanted to say Happy Father's Day!

Lovingly, Suz"

Eighteen words! Eighteen thousand words from another could never mean as much! I read them over and over and over and over again. I took a screen shot and began texting everyone. Joy, tears, disbelief, andrelief overwhelmed me as well as real anguish that I could not reply. My weary heart had that for which it had hungered, hope. I told Bob and Darlene that I would, indeed, be sitting in our usual place in the front and saving seats for them. I praised God for His goodness to everyone who would listen. I find it amazing how much good can come from a small kindness.

Also amazing is how quickly one can forget. Four days later as I was working from home, I became, as I phrased it in my journal, "paralyzed with grief." The fifty days I had been isolated was infinitely less of a sentence than I deserved, but my heart had so many reasons to grieve. God was changing me, and I knew that His grace was moving my life, but I had a world of hurt for which to apologize and a universe of debt to pay back to a woman who had shown real love.

The "Love Chapter" of the Bible is I Corinthians 13, and Matthew Henry explains the love or "charity" of I Corinthians 13 this way:

agape : not what is meant by charity in our common use of the word, which most men understand of alms—giving, but love in its fullest and most extensive meaning, true love to God and man, a benevolent disposition of mind towards our fellow-Christians, growing out of sincere and fervent devotion to God. This living principle of all duty and obedience is the more excellent way of which the apostle speaks, preferable to all gifts.

"Real love" is not what we muster from the paltry pantries of our own hearts, but it is what flows to others, from God and through us. This was love I had received. Have you ever asked yourself if you love someone and then measured it by God's definition?

• • *Charity suffereth long, and is kind.*

Suzanne had suffered my rage and anger for nearly thirty years, and she never ceased to be kind. Is that how you show love? I would beg any woman in Suzanne's position to get help at the first sign of rage, but in terms of love, would you be kind after thirty years of mistreatment?

• *Charity envieth not.*

Do you have the kind of love that does not feel, let alone show, jealousy? Are you willing to share the object of your love with those he/she loves?

• *Charity vaunteth not itself.*

Can you look back at your relationship with the one you love and honestly say that you have not promoted yourself? As a loving husband you would never say, "I am your husband, after all!" would you? Are you free from the need to push your loved one to love you in return?

• *Charity is not puffed up.*

In terms of your relationship, do you have a rather high opinion of yourself? Do you believe you have the right to occupy a certain place in the heart of your loved one? Do you believe he/she owes you a certain type of reciprocation?

• *Charity doth not behave itself unseemly.*

Pastor Bob floored me when he said he had never raised his voice to his wife. He is demonstrating a way in which he has not behaved himself unseemly. Could your loved one say, "Remember the time you…" or even "Remember the TIMES when you…?" Does your kind of love behave itself in an inappropriate, undignified manner?

• *Charity seeketh not her own.*

Would the object of your love consider you to be selfish?

• *Charity is not easily provoked.*

Exactly how hard is it to "push your buttons"? In all honesty, are you easily irritated?

• *Charity thinketh no evil.*

Before you know the details, do you assume the best or the worst of the one you love? If the phone rings from your child's school, do you say,

"What has he/she done now?" Do you presume motives upon the one you love?

- *Charity rejoiceth not in iniquity.*

Do you lead the one you love to do wrong? Does "having a little fun" or "living a little" include engaging in iniquity? Does the object of your love have to dip his or her sails a little to be with you?

- *Charity rejoiceth in the truth.*

If the one you love began to seek God fervently, with real zeal, would you be happy?

- *Charity beareth all things.*

My mind goes to my friend, Steve. Steve has lovingly cared for his wife after several strokes. He absolutely adores her! Steve's eyes light up at the mention of his lovely wife. He spends and is spent for Laurie. Does your spouse know that you would care for him or her the way Steve cares for Laurie?

- *Charity believeth all things; hopeth all things; endureth all things. Charity never faileth....*

Matthew Henry encourages Christians to see the verses with words such as these:

"... it is apt to believe well of all, to entertain a good opinion of them when there is no appearance to the contrary; nay, to believe well when there may be some dark appearances, if the evidence of ill be not clear. All charity is full of candor, apt to make the best of everything, and put on it the best face and appearance? It will judge well, and believe well, as far as it can with any reason, and will rather stretch its faith beyond appearances for the support of a kind opinion; And when, in spite of inclination, it cannot believe well of others, it will yet hope well, and continue to hope as long as there is any ground for it...Happy the man who has this heavenly fire glowing in his heart, flowing out of his mouth, and diffusing its warmth over all with whom he has to do! How lovely a thing would Christianity appear to the world, if those who profess it were more actuated and animated by this divine...Blessed Jesus! How few of thy professed disciples are to be distinguished and marked out by this characteristic!"

Perhaps one may see some of these points differently. Perhaps this author has missed the mark. Nevertheless, there are fair questions to be answered. How do I fare against my own I Corinthians 13 test? Do I LOVE? I must. I must love with a true love; there is no other way. I need to give that perfect love which casts out all fear. Fear has torment. Abuse and love cannot occupy the same place at the same time. Love. I must, by all means, *Walk in love, as Christ also hath loved us, and hath given himself for us an offering and a sacrifice to God for a sweet smelling savour* (Ephesians 5:2). Love is the only way.

Christians should take the I Corinthians love test with every interaction. While I, in my human state, will never ace the love test with a perfect score, I was almighty fond of a gal who never failed to make the honor roll.

The grief that paralyzed me was a mix of griefs. I was grieved selfishly at my own loneliness, I was grieved with the guilt of my endless list of hurtful actions; I was grieved at the brokenness of our relationship, and I was grieved that Suzanne was out of her element and not free to live her normal life. I was truly overwhelmed.

One might opine that this grief was an overreaction after seven weeks, but such an opinion would show a lack of understanding. Seven weeks apart was but the tip of my iceberg: I had grief for my wife; I had grief for my children; I had grief for severed and stalled relationships, and I had grief for what my sin had done to a loving Saviour. At one point, I got up from my desk, went into the prayer room, shut the door, and threw myself on the bed. I lay there tearfully staring at the ceiling. After a few moments I called out to the LORD, "I'm not calling anyone. I am not texting anyone. I am not reaching out to any human. My faith has to be in You. Whether or not I ever see her again, I need You. You have to be the One who comes through for me. Please help me."

With that said, I turned over and prayed very briefly for two friends who were undergoing chemotherapy. I wiped my tears and headed back to my work station. For some reason, when I left the prayer room, instead of turning left toward my desk, I turned right toward the back of the house. It was 12:30 p.m., and as I passed my wife's computer, I saw a Facebook notification. I saw that Suzanne had sent a note via her mother's Facebook account.

12:28PM

Just want to say that I love you. Looking forward to talking to you on our anniversary. Will probably call sometime on Sunday afternoon.

I realized that Suzanne had been typing at the exact same time that I was crying out to God. I recorded in my journal:

I have told this story many times today. Thank You, Jesus!

What I have not told *(others)* is that today I forgot to take my pills for only the second time since Suzanne left, and for the second time, I had an emotional wreck of a day.

God was so good to provide me both relief and further insight.

Thank You, Jesus.

It would seem logical to believe that part of my meltdown had been the added pain from missing the medications and from the fact that my medications had some antidepressant qualities. Whatever the source of the pain had been, my answer had come from God. This was not a holiday; nothing was special about the day at all. She had confirmed her love to me at exactly the time when I had needed it. God is a rewarder of those that diligently seek Him (Hebrews 11:6), and believing that is a big part of faith.

HOPEFUL HELPS

- Love.
- Trust God.
- God hears and answers a humble cry for help.
- Beware of pride.

Being Honest

Are you caught in the grip of rage and anger? Are you ensnared by some other vice or device? May I please suggest that you turn from flesh to faith? The Apostle Paul described this deliverance in Romans 7:14-25.

For we know that the law is spiritual: but I am carnal, sold under sin. For that which I do I allow not: for what I would, that do I not; but what I hate, that do I. If then I do that which I would not, I consent unto the law that it is good. Now then it is no more I that do it, but sin that dwelleth in me. For I know that in me (that is, in my flesh,) dwelleth no good thing: for to will is present with me; but how to perform that which is good I find not. For the good that I would I do not: but the evil which I would not, that I do. Now if I do that I would not, it is no more I that do it, but sin that dwelleth in me.

I find then a law, that, when I would do good, evil is present with me. For I delight in the law of God after the inward man: but I see another law in my members, warring against the law of my mind, and bringing me into captivity to the law of sin which is in my members. O wretched man that I am! who shall deliver me from the body of this death? I thank God through Jesus Christ our LORD....

In my flesh dwelleth no good thing. The strength of the human will has only the most temporal of help. True strength comes through the Spirit. He responds to faith. God is a rewarder. Seek Him diligently, for He says, *Without faith it is impossible to please him: for he that cometh to God must believe that he is, and that he is a rewarder of them that diligently seek him.* (Hebrews 11:6) Do you believe God? Seek Him.

On June 22 I had my seventh session with my psychotherapist. Steve operates from a Christian perspective. In most of our sessions, it seemed to be more than enough for Steve to keep up with the reports of work I had done with my three other counselors. He did give some feedback each week, and on this day, he recommended the book *Emotionally Healthy Spirituality* by Peter Scazzero.

I ordered the book from the parking lot of Steve's office. I found three helpful points in the book. Steve would later find that summary to be humorous and comment on my mission-oriented personality. The mission-oriented outlook is the opposite of what Mr. Scazzero is aiming for in his book. He wants to help readers find qualitative, rather than quantitative, success.

The thoughts that most helped my recovery were found in Chapter Eight's "Discover the Rhythms of the Daily Office and Sabbath" (Scazzero, 2017). The author enjoins the reader to take time each day to acknowledge God and to rest in the LORD. He gives principals, methods and examples. The chapter was helpful in the midst of my days as I moved through emotional and spiritual minefields between my morning prayer time and my evening prayer time.

Another benefit I found in the book was a skill which therapists think to be essential to life: a sharpening of an ability to recognize my own emotions. The concept is that at any given time a person should be able to identify his feelings and name them. Much of this approach was covered in Chapter 5, "Know Yourself That You May Know God," but is truly woven throughout the book.

The book also helped me to grow. It was written from a completely different doctrinal perspective than the very conservative Baptist theology which I had known since my teens. II Peter 1 does command that as a Christian, giving all diligence you should *add to your faith virtue* (v. 5). This strength of character does require setting doctrinal anchors and boundaries, but not all knowledge lies within the confines of my own worldview.

I had never read a book by someone with Scazzero's doctrinal tendencies, and though I wanted to learn Steve's lessons, I did not want to read the book. On June 25, I had a telephone conversation with my father, and we discussed how I was progressing. I mentioned to him the struggle I was having with doctrinal issues, and he rather sternly admonished me that my problems were not doctrinal problems.

That call did not go well. Other factors were also at work, but I was not ready to have someone close to me challenge what I knew to be true—at least not in this arena. People at peace are able to conduct respectful conversations. Respect would allow my dad to have his own opinion, virtue would hold me firm in my faith, and peace would allow me to conduct myself with joy. My response to Dad clearly showed that something was still missing.

Can people disagree with you without fear of an eruption? How about those closest to you? Does your spouse feel perfectly comfortable expressing an opinion that is diametrically opposed to yours? If not, why not? *God hath not given us the spirit of fear; but of power, and of love, and of a sound mind* (II Timothy 1:7).

Suzanne had confirmed that our anniversary call would actually happen and that she loved me. What was I to do? How would the call be? This was to be the first of weekly calls that would be for ten minutes each. How do I even begin to apologize for thirty years in ten minutes? Five minutes! She would deserve at least five minutes! I scripted it and had several people look at it. (God bless their patient souls!) What I intended to say is as follows:

Suzanne, you are the godliest, sweetest, most precious woman alive. My crimes against you are heinous. Anyone who knew one percent of what you have suffered would say you should never want to see me again. You are innocent; I am guilty.

My heart could not hurt more if it were dipped in boiling oil. Everything you said in the PFA complaint was true, but it did not scratch the surface of my crimes.

Thank you for having the courage to make a change. I owe you my life.

I grieve so deeply that you are better not to see me, not to hear me, and not to receive the expressions of love I long to give you. I grieve so deeply, but I believe in you and want you to have what you need for healing.

God has changed me. Should you ever want to hear my voice, you will hear love, acceptance, grace, and humility. I will take your call always and will do all I can to bless you.

I will never, ever hurt you again. Period. That is a vow.

If you decide to come home, you will be welcomed as my equal partner. We will build a NEW marriage on a godly foundation. We will work through my pride and selfishness to grow me into the husband you deserve.

I gave you 10,898 days of godless fear, and it is my prayer that I may give you 11,000 days of godly love and respect. (We'll have to start soon and live awhile, but it is my prayer.)

You are innocent; I thank you and owe you my life. I am so sorry.

Is there anything I can do for you?

What a great speech! What a heartfelt and sincere apology! What a bunch of meaningless mush. What my wife needed was not a dump truckload of sentiment dropped on her head; what she needed was some ability to communicate with me and learn about what had happened in the preceding months.

Why did I not stop and think about the questions she might have? Was my perspective the only perspective? Did she want an apology or a list of promises? I had much to learn. Listening is hard; talking is easy. A woman who wants reconciliation needs to know that she has a voice. A man who has harmed his wife can only learn the depths of the hurts from her. Listening is hard, but necessary.

The pastor and I were in constant communication in those days and met a couple of times each week. At one point, he seemed to believe that there would be no time limit on the first phone call and that no second party would be joining the call. Later he learned that there would be some time limit. We would not, he told me, speak for an hour. Pastor Wilkerson had told me that she wanted the call to be on our anniversary and that she wanted it to be sweet.

I did not know where she was going to call, and by the order of the PFA, I could not ask anyone to ask her. How was I to know where to go? Was she calling Pastor's phone? He was listed on the PFA as someone who could listen on my behalf. Would she call my phone directly? I would have done whatever she asked, but my hope was that she would call me on my phone. I wanted to go to West Virginia, to get away from my seemingly haunted home, and to spend some time with a family I loved dearly.

For twenty-one of our twenty-nine years, Suzanne and I had lived in the same house. Those years were bathed in memories of love and laughter that magnified the sense of loss. There were also memories of anger and wrath that magnified the sense of guilt and responsibility. At different times, I had hidden every picture of Suzanne simply to avoid those memories. By late June, not only had I put them back up, but I had also added many others. However, I still wanted to get out of my homemade haunted house.

On Wednesday night, June 25, Pastor Wilkerson told me what to expect. She would call my phone sometime between 3:00 p.m. and 5:00 p.m. CST. Glory to God! I could go to West Virginia!

Craig and Debbie were real friends, and my time with them was delightful. We were constantly busy about the business of his pastoring the church. On Saturday morning, we went to a men's prayer breakfast followed by a visitation meeting for the whole church. From there we went to see the property where his new church building was slated to be built. Later we made some pastoral visits for the church. Craig and Debbie were the blessings of the trip.

Ointment and perfume rejoice the heart: so doth the sweetness of a man's friend by hearty counsel...

Verse 17:*Iron sharpeneth iron; so a man sharpeneth the countenance of his friend.* (Proverbs 27:9,17)

Discussing a tear in the fabric of your family with family members is hard. Certain topics cannot be addressed well with family members, so hours spent with true friends can be true treasures.

HOPEFUL HELPS

- In our flesh is no good thing; we must live in the Spirit.
- We sin with our whole being; our whole being needs help.
- Let us look at our sin from the perspective of those we have hurt.
- Beware of pride.

Starting Over

Our anniversary fell on a Sunday afternoon. Pastor Wilkerson had informed me that the call would probably come sometime between two o'clock and three o'clock. I read, re-read, and adjusted my tiny script. I watched and watched and watched the phone until it vibrated. The caller ID displayed "Unknown Caller."

"This is it!" I said as I bolted to the basement bedroom that was my weekend home. I fumbled the earbuds into my ears, plugged the cord into the phone, and answered. I had practiced my greeting more times than I would like to admit. "Well, hello, Beautiful," I said in the deepest, most sultry voice I could muster. Then I started into my speech, flying through the words like a child trying to spit out memorized lines.

She interrupted me and said that there were a few items she needed to start with. She told me that she loved me and that she had chosen our anniversary as the day for the first call because it was such a special day. She went on to say that we would start having ten-minute phone calls every Tuesday night, starting on July 11.

She went on to say that she had been seeing a professional counselor and had read several books on abusive anger. All pointed to there being a cycle of abuse. "It will take time," she told me, "to prove to me and to certain family members that your words are not just part of that cycle." She continued with some quotes that she believed were germane to my redemption. She said that our relationship needed to be based on honesty without fear of retaliation.

That phone call was great and terrible, wonderful and awful, happy and heart-crushing. Suzanne has THE best phone voice anywhere. Her tones are usually pleasant, but that voice was not there that day. Suzanne said all the right words in exactly the wrong voice.

I promised her that if she were to drop the protection order nothing would change. I would still provide financial support, and would respect her needs for healing and space. I would leave communication completely in her control. Dropping the order would simply give us more options. That effort went south in a hurry, and my words would return to haunt me.

A mutual moderator could have made that call a lot better. Nobody on my end heard the conversation, so no one could tell me what actually happened. The protection order had stipulated that only three people could join a call on my behalf, and none of them were available in West Virginia.

A godly woman does not flee her home lightly. It had been a big and painful decision. Suzanne had risked everything she held dear in the hope of finding something she had never seen. She had left without saying her goodbyes to our son and daughter-in-law. Her dear friends of a lifetime had sent texts asking about her whereabouts. She had left her church, her ministries, her home, and the future for which she had worked. She had left with no income and no retirement plan. As hard as it was for me to understand, she had left a man she had given the best years of her life.

That life she sought, that life she had never seen before was a peaceful, caring, and godly home. She had walked into the darkness of separation hoping to find the light of love. When she dialed my phone number on July 2, what would she have hoped to hear? Would a woman in her position take such a drastic journey and pay such a high price only to come to such a moment for bargaining? Would a godly woman use her marriage as a bargaining chip? Of course not.

A man who comes to his first chance at reconciliation might do well to learn from my mistakes. Love does not look like a bargaining session. It looks like Jesus coming forward to sacrifice himself. Jesus did not come to earth to play "Let's Make a Deal!"

So much had happened in the two months since Suzanne had left. God had effected so many changes in my heart, and He had shown me so many kindnesses by the hands of His people. I had wept so many tears, prayed so many prayers, read so many books, and sought in so many directions for truth. Any account of such things could have ministered grace to lady who so richly deserved to see it.

Most men whose wives leave after abuse will never have a chance to reconcile. For those blessed with such an opportunity, they would do well to come to the call ready to give and not take. Suzanne left because she needed to see the security of love spring from the ashes of pride.

If I read statistics accurately, only about eight percent of couples who are separated after abuse reconcile at all. I have not been able to find statistics on how many of those reconciliations are long-lasting or happy. It may well be that many or most women would do well to forever avoid their abusers, but what of those families that can be saved?

Calls like these are difficult at best. Moderators are such a benefit! An objective third party can shed much light on such difficult situations. Is your church willing to spend the time and money to have people such as adult Sunday school teachers attend something similar to the Chris Moles project "Peaceworks University"? Do you have professional counselors who might benefit from "Equip," the joint venture between Chris and Leslie Vernick? Trained servants provide better service.

Just as I found with the book *Emotionally Healthy Spirituality*, not all help comes from those who dot every ecclesiastical "i" and cross every ecclesiastical "t" exactly as I do. There are sources secular and sacred to which one must avail himself or herself to avoid the damage done by novices. Beware; novices should not operate in this space alone. Anyone can volunteer to help, but neither my opinion nor theirs can protect the abused.

Such a small percentage of couples reunite after the wife departs an abusive situation! For those who do reunite, there is an increased risk to women returning after abuse. Without question, couples attempting to see this miracle need the help of a loving church. Is your church such a church? Are you willing? Will you do what is necessary to be helpful rather than just be involved? There is a difference.

The next day I had my first call with Chris Moles. Chris began to walk down a very specific journey by taking me through Biblical perspectives of the roots of sin, responsibility, and other carefully chosen subjects. Some of the questions were piercing and personal, but then, so were the acts I had committed. This, too, would become an important part of my future.

As much as I might have liked to jump straight to the next step, much of life is made up of the mundane routines. After hanging up on that first call, I had nine days to live with the LORD until my next opportunity to communicate with Suzanne. Along the way I attended a cancer benefit for a courageous miracle of grace named Melinda, exercised daily, and continued walking with God. I could not prove to myself, my counselors, Suzanne, or her family in any one day or week that I was ready to move forward. Growth is a process, and I needed to *grow in grace, and in the knowledge of our LORD and Saviour Jesus Christ.* (II Peter 3:18).

Interestingly, my pastor was actually born on the Fourth of July, and this year marked his fiftieth birthday. The church hosted a July 4 birthday celebration and a church picnic in his honor. I went and enjoyed the company. On my way out a long-time church member stopped me and said, "I've seen Suzanne's pictures on Facebook! It looks like she is having a wonderful time! When is she coming back?"

I still did not know how to answer that one gracefully, so I replied, "Suzanne left me."

I heard the same answer I had heard many times: "You're kidding!"

Why does everyone say the same thing!? I wondered. "No. Didn't you hear my Mother's Day confession to the church? She left me after thirty years of abusive anger at home. I have no idea if or when she will come back."

The blank stare of disbelief was followed by a quick explanation of the fact that their family had been out of town on Mother's Day. Tears flowed, and I walked away in shame, grief, and horror. God knows how to humble those who will not humble themselves. The sandpaper of reality was still smoothing away the coarseness of my soul.

On July 9, Pastor and I went over my July 2 call with Suzanne. He was encouraging and kind and helped me to look at life through God's eyes. The next day I had lunch with a friend whose husband had gone to jail for abusing her. They were separated for six months and had lived through a hellish first year of reunification. She gave me insights on Suzanne's needs for future calls. On the morning of July 11, the day of my first official, ten-minute call with Suzanne, I met with my therapist, and he also gave me advice on how to approach the call.

Both my therapist and my lady friend had the same perspective. Suzanne needed empathetic listening. I needed to ask her about her hurts and her feelings. She needed the freedom to tell me safely about how I had hurt her and about her needs now. I made notes and prepared for the call to come. I was ready. The time came for her call, and I waited, and I waited and waited.

HOPEFUL HELPS

- Abuse is a prevalent problem; "people helpers" need knowledge and training.
- Listen.
- Beware of pride.

Shedding Water

The phone rang! Once again I put on my deepest, sexiest voice and gave my best "Hello, Beautiful. Where have YOU been all my life?" She chuckled sheepishly and said her hellos. "I know we only have ten minutes."

Suzanne interrupted me and told me that she had forgotten to tell me that we would not have such a time limit. Other people were involved in waiting for us, so we would need to keep it under an hour, but there would be no strict ten-minute limit. After hearing from Suzanne, I started with my empathetic listening questions. Suzanne was not having it—not that she was rude or refused to answer the questions, she simply had nothing much to say. She showed no internal need for the discussion. A day would come in Colorado Springs, Colorado, when I would begin to understand the reasons.

This call was a much better call. Both of us were still a bit scripted, but I avoided asking for any changes, and Suzanne's voice softened quite a bit. We talked about what was going on in our individual lives, though Suzanne was still somewhat guarded. She did want to know how things were going with my counselors and with Chris, in particular.

Most of what Chris and I had worked on centered on taking inventory of what had happened. We looked at lists of behaviors in abusive homes, lists of behaviors in our home, impacts of different kinds of harmful actions, and the comparison of these harmful patterns to healthy patterns. I was in the process of completing an exercise in which I was to take specific responsibility for my actions toward Suzanne.

I told Suzanne that Chris asked extremely pointed questions and that I was working on a homework assignment that was a letter to her, taking responsibility for my actions. I told her that it was a very hard set of words to write and that the words would be very hard to hear. She wanted to hear it. In one of our upcoming calls, Suzanne wanted to hear every word.

Geographically, a watershed is a piece of high ground, typically a ridge, where water on one side of the ridge drains in a different direction than the water on the other side of the ridge. The Great Divide is the watershed that separates the water which flows to the Atlantic from the water that flows to the Pacific. There is an exact spot on the map where it changes. From Cape Prince, Alaska, in the north to the Occidental Mountains of Mexico in the south, a person can stand with one foot on either side of the Great Divide. Atlantic or Pacific? Fast-moving water or slow-moving water? It is your watershed; you decide!

The week of July 9, 2017, was a watershed for our marriage. Reconciliation? Quick reunion or long process? Divorce? Fast and painless (if such exists) or slow and excruciating? The water of our lives would begin to flow this week; this was our "Great Divide." We did not know that it would happen, we did not know that it was happening, and we would not know for months what had happened, but this was it.

Oddly enough, the first step toward resolution was resignation. A person would think that his destiny lies in choosing to choose and deciding to decide, but such was not my case. On Wednesday night, I went to church as I would for any other midweek service. The pastor taught an overview of the book of Leviticus. Sounds life-changing, right? For me, it was.

Somewhere in addressing the feasts, the concept of surrendering my will to God's will became clear. It seems self-evident. He is God; He is Sovereign. He knows best; He loves me. Plainly I should trust Him for the details of my life, and I should give up my own pursuit of outcomes and methods. I had not done so.

That night when I went to bed, I did not sleep. I repeatedly prayed through the night, "LORD, I need You. LORD, I need YOU." Somewhere around 2:30 a.m., I turned over on my face and gave my will to God. If it was to be reconciliation, I was fine with His plan and His timeline. If I had forfeited my privilege to have Suzanne in my life, I would trust Him to take me to the right place in life. To reach the watershed, I had to shed my own will.

Coming to this point was the second of four changes in my life on the path to hope. There was, indeed, hope for me. My hope was in the LORD Who made Heaven and earth. My heart was fixed, trusting in Him. I could not put a finger on it, but life was different. *But without faith it is impossible to please hime: for he that cometh to God MUST believe that He is, and that He is a rewarder of those that diligently seek Him.* (Hebrews 11:6) I believed, and I was seeking anew.

The just shall live by faith is found in Galatians 3:11 and three other passages. Every child of God begins the path to peace at the point of surrender.

On Saturday evening I was scheduled to have a call with Suzanne and Pastor Wilkerson on his phone at the Bible college operated by our church. I met him about half an hour before the call, and we planned the sorts of words we would say. I had worked on the topics that would be meaningful to me, and I would soon find that Suzanne had done the same.

The phone rang. "Hello, Beautiful! And how may I minister to you tonight?"

She responded with a blushing giggle. That response seemed good. "By being just real with me," Suzanne replied in her normal voice. "How was your day? What's going on in your life?"

I told Suzanne about helping a friend move belongings, soul winning with Bob, and homework with Chris. I then attempted to explain the change that God had made in my life on Wednesday night. Spiritual transformation is hard to explain, and I failed miserably. She brushed it off.

My attitude, however, was contrite. With tears I explained that the abuse had been all about me and that the restoration was to be all about her. I told my wife that I did not intend to control any agenda. Her response, in a word, was skeptical.

Suzanne went on to tell me about her own spiritual transformation. She had focused in recent days on the Biblical term *lovingkindness*, referenced Psalm 88:11, and then turned her attention to Psalm 66:3, which says, *Because thy lovingkindness is better than life, my lips shall praise thee.* She continued by saying that she believed she had exhibited a lack of respect for me in our marriage because I had exhibited a lack of lovingkindness. Kindness makes praise real instead of fake.

She went on to mention that I had offered her a gift during our previous call when I had suggested that she could order a bicycle that I had saved in our shared Amazon account and that I would pay for it. Suzanne explained that did not believe that such a gift was in keeping with the protection order, and furthermore, she and others thought that gift giving was part of a cycle of abuse.

Suzanne told me that if she could put gifts on one side and kindness on the other, she would choose both! If she could only choose one, she would choose kindness. She realized there had been a lack of respect in our marriage, but she also opined that respect must be earned to be real. Had I shown lovingkindness, she could have grown respect for me.

This was the progress we needed. We were moving towards marital honesty without selfishness, but I was not mature enough to recognize it. I was cornered and worried. My voice became slow and stilted. I responded that she was right. I had been harsh instead of kind. I spoke in a slow, awkward voice about the future.

Suzanne continued, "Anger is a cycle. It is breakable." Then she added, "Thanks for all you have done," and "I think you have done all you can do." She reaffirmed her belief that gift giving was part of the abuse cycle, and that the lessons we were learning would take time to take root and grow.

We needed time—time to move forward. The water of our lives seemed to be breaking toward Reconciliation River, but my loneliness reached down, grabbed my foot, and shoved it into my mouth. "We need time," I said, "But we have already spent a quarter of a year apart. Only eight-to-ten percent of couples in our situation get back together, and all of this time apart can be damaging."

Damaging? What kind of description is that? I had promised not to try to control any agenda, but there I was—pushing. I continued in an increasingly harsh tone that the protection order was worthless. I asserted that we needed to communicate and that I would respect her wishes. Was I, at that moment, respecting her wishes? No, not at all.

I pressed forward, admonishing her that reading I Corinthians 6 would make the protection go away. "Not all conversations," I opined, "needed to be about hard things. We need time to speak to each other lovingly." I stopped to breathe.

"Will you get counsel when necessary when I come home?"

"WHEN I COME HOME?"

Water was clearly flowing, though it was slow.

I answered with a commitment I had already made to Pastor Wilkerson, "I am willing to seek counsel at any level you believe I or we need it for the rest of our lives. You are a different person now; you are my partner." I continued to share that on May 5 and the following day, I had learned the root of my sin—satanic and idolatrous pride. "The root has been pulled out," I declared. Of course, that sentiment was a bit premature. Pride plagues us throughout life and can only be conquered in Heaven. I wanted to be rid the plague, but that work had only begun.

We went on to discuss counselors and Suzanne's need for assurances from Steve and Chris that home was safe. I explained how and what both could provide and told her that I was continuing with all four of my counselors.

Suzanne referred again to my confession before the church. Little did I know that Suzanne had it on her phone and that she watched it often. The decision I had feared making without her input was one of the biggest blessings to her and one of the primary sources feeding the headwaters of our Reconciliation River. Merely a trickle of water was flowing on July 15 as it ran through the rocks of our relationship above the tree line of hope, but it was real, and it was flowing.

The process of recovering from trauma is not like applying a Band-Aid. The recovery is more like physical therapy when a person learns anew to walk and talk. Anyone in such a situation could use a good, strong dose of Jeremiah 9:24, which says: *But let him that glorieth glory in this, that he understandeth and knoweth me, that I am the LORD which exercise lovingkindness, judgment, and righteousness, in the earth: for in these things I delight, sayeth the LORD.*

If a real marriage were to rise from the traumatic ashes of our disaster, it would have to be a miracle. I did not have, nor could I find, the wisdom and understanding necessary for such a transformation. In all the chaos of the deep wounds (Though Suzanne was the victim, we both had wounds.), I could see only one way: we needed the blessings of God. We needed to exercise the lovingkindness, judgment, and righteousness one to the other that the LORD had toward each of us.

The conversation turned to the fact that Suzanne had heard through the grapevine that I was considering a dog—a sweet, little Boerboel named Kona. As Boerboel Mastiffs go, she was small, tilting the scales around 130 pounds. Boerboels are not slow, lumbering mastiffs. They are the kind that guard herds in Africa from lions. Kona was a sweetheart, and for days when the house was empty, she had all that was needed to keep it safe. She could stand on all fours and look out the front door with her massive head and issue a bark that reaches to the bones. Kona was perfect for me *if I were alone.*

Suzanne hates slobbering dogs. Strike one. She loves dogs that are hypoallergenic and do not shed. Strike two. Suzanne's dog, Mocha, would fit neatly in Kona's mouth. Strike three. While we were both cordial about the matter of Kona, she made too much of the issue, and I made too much of the issue. Such is the way of a marriage gasping for breath.

Kona, if perfect for me, was not perfect for our marriage. I assured Suzanne that I would not adopt the dog. I further assured her that she was my priority and that such issues would not become obstacles.

As we shifted back to the relationship, I wanted Suzanne to know that the changes in my life were permanent. I walked her through my walk with God, the ways that my actions and attitudes were different, and my understanding of how I had allowed myself to commit such awful acts.

For decades I had told her how I admired her spirit, and on this day I defined that admiration for her. "I love your spirit, Suzanne. This week I believe I have defined it. You have a little '*h*,' holy spirit."

She gasped at my words.

I went on to say that I believed her heart belonged to the LORD. I added, "I do not want to fix our old marriage; I want a new marriage."

Suzanne responded that her family was protective and that they would have a hard time trusting me. "It will take time, but that time can come." Parenthetically, Suzanne asked me if I would continue to treat her family with jealousy. I promised that I would not.

After some details about our schedules, my heart began to spew itself across the airwaves. "I can't tell you how much I love you. I long to give you a head massage or hold your hand [she giggled], or see the twinkle in your eyes. I long to take you for grilled vegetables and a pizza. I want to hear your laugh or see you smile. I know that I have caused so much harm…I can never even understand the harm I've caused. There is not a moment of my life when I don't wish to God that I had done something different."

I thank the LORD for giving me the pain, and the drugs, and the things that made it bad enough that you had to leave…I needed Jesus. If I had to choose between you and Jesus, I would choose Jesus." This statement was true, and my saying it was evidence to myself, if to no one else, that I was changing."

My words that day might lead one to believe that I was blaming God for the abuse I visited upon my wife. In the ebb and flow of conversations, there are many concepts that never rise to the surface. I could not have told Suzanne God's purposes for my trials any more than Job could have told his wife God's purpose for the boils that covered his body. I was thankful that God had used those circumstances for our benefit, but I was and am deeply grieved at the sin itself.

"You're precious! You're beautiful! You deserve respect. I keep hearing about men who do not respond in this situation as I have. I don't know who these other people are, but they (*had not lived with my perspective*). If they had, they would do anything they could to give you back what I've stolen from you."

My wife responded with a tender voice, "I love you, too…I still mean everything I said in that letter…I believe in you…I am so thankful that God chose us to be husband and wife, that you are getting counsel, and that I have time here. He's been showing me that He is very loving and very kind…I know the LORD is here, and He is with me. He has allowed this time for a purpose."

It got better after that. "I believe in you. I love you very much. I am so excited that we are both willing to make our marriage work. We are on the right track. We are doing what we know to do." I was thrilled.

Suzanne asked if we could pray together before we closed. Our half hour had become nearly an hour. She closed the conversation with the intent to enjoy time with family, and I went back to the empty house.

I had heard our conversation with the ear of hope, but Suzanne had listened to me through the headphones of hurt and fear. She heard my stilted voice and thought it sounded phony. Later I would learn that she would text the pastor that same day and ask him if he had thought that I was being real.

HOPEFUL HELPS

- Forgiveness heals.
- Marriage requires honesty without selfishness.
- God exercises lovingkindness, judgment, and righteousness; it is His delight when we exercise them with each other.
- Recovery takes time and effort.
- Beware of pride.

Losing Phil

Suzanne had made it her practice to have someone in Maine listen when she and I talked on the phone. I am glad she did. On July 15, however, she had relied solely on Pastor Wilkerson. This date marked a softening of Suzanne's heart and an expression of trust. But not all progress is pleasant.

When some folks who love Suzanne very much found out that she had talked with me while alone, their fears created conflict, and that conflict grew. In a family meeting, feelings were aired. Many of our loved ones did not approve of our church and were quite vocal about it that Saturday night. Suzanne did have an ally in her friend, Laura, but the tension was real, and so were the consequences. It was decided that it would be better for Suzanne to live under a different roof than to make decisions about our relationship that did not meet with family approval. Such is the way for conflict born of fear.

One might think that people aiding an abuse victim would be slow to dole out consequences. If you are ever in that position, would you be willing to suspend your judgmental tendencies? Can you, as I have often quoted, be "gentle, apt to teach, in meekness instructing?" Please do. Victimized adults do not need guardians; they need the loving support of friends and family.

Recently I have watched some foxes growing up in the backyard of our home. A fox kit will not learn to hunt until its mother refuses to let it nurse. Some animals will not leave the nest until the nest becomes uncomfortable. On July 15, an important place of refuge in Maine became less comfortable for Suzanne. Her loved ones failed to learn a primary lesson of abuse which was that one cannot impose his or her will on another. That is God's domain, and He seldom imposes Himself. For example, in marriage, a couple is to submit themselves *one to another in the fear of God* (Ephesians 5:21).

Spiritual recovery is not played out entirely on earth. Job had no notion of what was happening in Heaven while his life fell apart; Daniel did not see the clash of angels while he prayed, nor do we have a clue today what is going on in the spiritual backdrop of our lives. God's purpose in every blessing is to make His child more like Christ.

Later that day I posted a link to a Spotify song being sung by Josh Wilson:

My Life Is Yours to Control
By Rodney and Jimmelynn Rice
(Used by permission)

With my whole heart I humbly seek you;
Now use my life, O LORD, I pray.
I yield my stubborn will completely;
May your commandments light my way.
Chorus
My life, LORD, is yours to control;
I give You my heart and my soul.

I'll seek Your will, never mine, Rich treasure to find.
Give wisdom to choices I make, Along ev'ry path that I take.
So when I complete life's race, "Well done," You will say.
Your Word has promised me the vict'ry,
And all I need to do is claim Your strength to soar with wings as eagles,
To walk, to run, and not to faint.

That morning during my prayer time, I looked up the song and downloaded it so that I could sing it to the LORD as a prayer during my morning walk with God. Day by day as I spent huge amounts of time alone with the LORD, He was teaching me, transforming me, and carefully molding my life as the Master Potter with a lump of clay.

A song I posted later was Keith Getty and Stuart Townsend's "The Perfect Wisdom of Our God." From the aching of my heart, hearing Mrs. Getty sing about the place of sorrows in the artwork of God's grace struck a chord in my heart. I felt as if I was hearing the echo of my own heart. On earth the time of my separation from Suzanne trudged on like an uphill mud hike through a cold, autumn rain. However in the heavenly places where we sit with Christ, life was moving at the speed of light. In very deed, life was being sped along by the ...*true Light, which lighteth every man that cometh into the world* (John 1:9).

Back on earth, July 22 was a lesson in miscommunication. I wrote to one of my counselors that "Suzanne anticipates an early November date for dropping the order of protection." Suzanne had said that she wanted to keep it in place for six months from May 3, which would mean November 3. A friend at church winked at me and said, "Suzanne wants to be back together for Thanksgiving." I had heard a commitment. I journaled, "As of yesterday we have a timeline in view—at least a bit of one."

That same day I journaled that, "We often sound more like lawyers negotiating terms than like lovers working to rebuild." This observation was especially true of our scheduled calls without a counselor. Counselors and mentors are beyond helpful during any important transition of life. These—not guardians—are the ones the victim needs in her corner. God establishes this fact at least three times in the Proverbs:

Where no counsel is, the people fall: but in the multitude of counsellors there is safety (11:14).

Without counsel purposes are disappointed: but in the multitude of counsellors they are established (15:22).

For by wise counsel thou shalt make thy war: and in multitude of counsellors there is safety (24:6).

In January of 1981, God gave me the kind of mentor never to be forgotten. That month I passed my driver's test, and with my shiny new license, I began to attend Calvary Baptist Church in Odessa, Texas. Almost immediately I joined the bus ministry and the bus route of Phil Winn.

Phil was a larger-than-life, bold, cheerful Texan. Every Saturday we would visit the bus route together, and I would watch that young man engage families with the hard issues of life. I was privileged to see his boldness in soul winning and his kindness for everyone. He stood fast on the Word of God as his anchor in all that he did.

On Sundays Phil and his sweet wife, Linda, would have me and others over to their house for lunch after we dropped off all of the kids. I was the one teen working on the bus route whose parents did not attend the church. My drive home was long enough that going home for the afternoon and driving back to Odessa for the evening service made little sense.

Phil was there for everything. I was not much younger than he was, but I imitated him more than I knew. He taught me to show people the Gospel, to be bold for God, and to do what I could to help.

I moved away from Texas just two and a half years later, but for many years he and I kept in touch. He stayed in my Indiana home many times during conferences. One year Suzanne and I took a road trip to the church he was pastoring. We saw the same old Phil living the same old way—

serving God boldly and simply.

On July 27, Phil Winn did something I had never anticipated. He died—with just a few days between diagnosis and death. I was stunned and hurt by the news; I was alone, and I wanted Suzanne to be with me. I wanted to put my arm around her and weep as I told her stories she had already heard too many times. It was against the law for me to contact her; I could not ask another to have her call me. That morning as I prayed, I told the LORD I needed human comfort.

God is sovereign, and He knew where I was. The times in life when we cast ourselves helplessly and completely upon Him are the times when He shows us what Jeremiah meant when he lamented, *It is of the LORD's mercies that we are not consumed, because his compassions fail not. They are new every morning: great is thy faithfulness.* (Lamentations 3:22, 23).

As God knew it would be, I had just adopted the kind of dog with which Suzanne was fine. This small, lively, 12-pound bundle of affection named Charlie needed a license. I left the house that afternoon to run some errands, and the first was to City Hall. I found my way to the right line and approached the window for my paperwork. I was happy to find out that registration was only seven dollars but dismayed to learn that the smallest credit payment was ten dollars. I had no cash.

A lady leaving the window next to me stepped past her two small children and said, "I'll pay for your dog." That gesture of kindness is exactly what Phil would have done. In the briefest terms, I told her so, and this perfect stranger gave me a big warm, bear hug. His compassions fail not; great is His faithfulness. That display of kindness and the ensuing hug were what I needed. Sometimes I hug anyone who does not get out of my way. (Not really, but sort of…) Hours after my prayer for human comfort God answered through the kindness of a young, random family.

HOPEFUL HELPS

- Adult victims of abuse require gentle, godly help—not guardians to control them.
- God's mercies are new every morning; seek Him.
- Beware of pride.

Taking Stock

In the work of reconciliation, what we needed most was the blessing of God. So many events were happened that fourth week of July that there was no way to chronicle them or to point out the importance of what God was doing. The metamorphosis of a butterfly happens in secret but is seen on the surface. So it was with me. My times of prayer and meditation, the impact of counselors, and the influence of books were all working within me, but the change was leaking out. Here, for example, is a Facebook post from that week:

> What happened to Jim?
>
> Romans 2:1-5 *Therefore thou art inexcusable, O man, whosoever thou art that judgest: for wherein thou judgest another, thou condemnest thyself; for thou that judgest doest the same things. But we are sure that the judgment of God is according to truth against them which commit such things. And thinkest thou this, O man, that judgest them which do such things, and doest the same, that thou shalt escape the judgment of God? Or despisest thou the riches of his goodness and forbearance and longsuffering; not knowing that the goodness of God leadeth thee to repentance? But after thy hardness and impenitent heart treasurest up unto thyself wrath against the day of wrath and revelation of the righteous judgment of God.*
>
> A hard, impenitent heart was beating proudly in my chest. I was so proud that I thought I was humble. In my wrongdoing, I believed myself justified, but God had given me notice. Do you ever accuse anyone else of pride? I did, and verse one gave me my warning. I did not know that the goodness of God was leading me to repentance until I repented.
>
> When I look at another with a critical eye, I can be sure I am really looking at my own sin. In case after case, that which I accused others of was, in fact, what I needed to address in my own life. Repentance is hard work. If you have judged or accused, may I suggest starting on repentance sooner rather than later? I wish I had, and I thank God that His goodness has indeed led me. The work in me is far from done.
>
> If you have ever prayed for me, please continue and so much the more.
>
> Thanks for indulging me with this long, awkward post.

Saturday, July 29, was another phone call where Suzanne and I had my pastor as our counselor, but she had seen another counselor named John Regier all week. John is the founder of Caring for the Heart Ministries and is the author of its curriculum. Suzanne had spent her entire previous week,

Monday through Friday, from 8:00 a.m. until 5:00 p.m., learning from John and his staff about counseling people with their hurts. She had purchased material and had learned much.

I started with "Hello" instead of a flirt that she might think sounded phony. She said that she had been looking forward to the phone call and followed that statement with, "I love you very, very much. I am excited about talking to you, and I have had an amazing week…I think that is a 'God thing' that I have had this week." She definitely touched my heart.

She briefly mentioned the conference and then offered her condolences for Phil's death. Reconciliation River was growing in depth, breadth, and speed. The size was still less than a creek, but it was visible and moving.

This day was also the wedding day of a young friend of Suzanne's who had gone on a missionary trip to Puerto Rico with her. They had become buddies, and Suzanne had been scheduled to speak at the bridal shower but had missed because of her escape to Maine. Suzanne asked me to sign the card for the two of us. The river was forming indeed.

Suzanne asked me to give her my testimony from childhood up until the time I left for college. I did not know that it was related to her conference. I gave my life story to my wife. Providentially, my tears flowed as I recalled some of the harder details of my childhood. Suzanne asked me if those memories continued to hurt me, haunt me, or affect me.

Both my testimony and the subsequent conversation came from my heart in a voice that was not stilted. Both of us talked in very open and honest tones. I was open; she was compassionate.

Suzanne told me what she had learned about herself at the conference. She discovered that she also had inner hurts. Some of them contributed to her attraction to me in spite of her concerns regarding my controlling nature and the singular episode of anger. "I didn't care about the other things so much because you loved me," she said.

In tears and with some sobs, she related, "I want you to know that I love you, and it had never, ever been my intention to leave you. I felt like I needed to get to a safe place so that I could understand what was happening in our marriage. I know that you did a lot better for some years but you (*did the thing that convinced her she needed to leave*). Sometimes when you live with anger, you don't necessarily see it as much—even if it hurts when it happens. I'm really glad for that reason that I did a very hard thing in leaving for a while."

She continued with tears in broken sentences and mixed thoughts. "I married you for better, for worse, for richer, for poorer, in sickness and in health...maybe this is just what I'm supposed to take to be like Christ... *I knew that* God was going to have to be the One to fix it..."

On Thursday night of the conference, Suzanne told the main speaker, John Regier, that she was in Maine because she had separated from me. He told her that he would be willing to see me for an entire week in his office in Colorado Springs. She asked if I would be willing to go either alone or with her. She said she could go to the court and ask to have the order changed to permit a week together for counseling.

In a heartfelt way, I again apologized for the hurt that I had given her. I told her that I was thankful she had left and that I was thankful we were "going to get things fixed." I committed to go and asked Suzanne to consider dropping the protection order outright so that we could be together in whatever setting the counselor saw fit. I told her that I had seventeen vacation days left and that all I cared to do with them was to become the man she needed me to be.

We talked about logistics, and I further committed to go whether she changed the order and whether or not she joined me. WOW! What a thought! Counseling together for a week in November. My heart was humbled beyond words. Even if she did not join me, the notion of counseling together was a clear sign that something had obviously changed her heart. I was 'all in' all over again, and my heart began to flow through my mouth.

"I would not be here if I had not come home and found a note on the table. I could have lived my entire life in carnal pride, hiding behind fleshly coping mechanisms that had nothing to do with the Spirit of God if you hadn't stood up and left." I went on to express my heart of real repentance.

As we moved toward the end of our call, Suzanne said in soft sobs and a cracking voice, "Our call today was amazing. Your attitude is very kind and gracious, and I appreciate that." We prayed in closing, and I told her the story of the lady at the license branch. I teased her that with my super-short hair and long beard, I had become a "chick magnet" and that she needed to get home. I also told her that the gal was attractive. "The women are just coming! It was a squeezy hug and everything!"

She laughed. "I hope it was my prayers that sent that total stranger to you. Just your attitude and the things we have talked about have truly shown me your love. I can't tell you how much I thank you for this time. I love you."

What a call! Reconciliation River was now at creek stage and flowing freely.

HOPEFUL HELPS

- The primary need in a work of restoration (or any spiritual endeavor) is the blessing of God.
- Be loving and considerate.
- Actions speak louder than words.
- Beware of pride.

Raising Gallows

Charity suffereth long, and is kind; charity envieth not; charity vaunteth not itself, is not puffed up, doth not behave itself unseemly, seeketh not her own, is not easily provoked, thinketh no evil; rejoiceth not in iniquity, but rejoiceth in the truth; beareth all things, believeth all things, hopeth all things, endureth all things. Charity never faileth... (I Corinthians 13:4-8).

Four days—August 2–5—marked a time of revealing a selfish, immature love in me that needed growth. What Suzanne needed was a confirmation of love. Without love, and with the horrid history she and I had, my carefully crafted words and clever conversations were sounding brass. In those four days, I had shown Suzanne, Pastor Wilkerson, and myself that my love was too easily provoked, that it was tainted with selfishness, and that it was not seasoned to bear, believe, hope, and endure.

On the first of those four days, Suzanne and I had a regularly scheduled, 29-minute call. We discussed the details of what I had learned about Caring for the Heart and John Regier's counseling ministry. Suzanne pulled back from her position of just three days earlier. Now she was talking about my trip but was not at all sure that she would attend the session in November. I mentioned that I was surprised, as the counseling session would be after November 3. The reference did not matter. After pleasantries, Suzanne was clear that she was not ready to confirm.

I became worried that this reversal was significant. Immediately after that call, I wrote the following to the pastor:

Good afternoon,

Thank you so much for your kindness and time for Suzanne and me.

I am concerned with one of the outcomes of my call last night. The first time that I can go to Colorado Springs is November 13-17. That is ten days after Suzanne talked about dropping the PFA. Even so, she is quite reticent to commit to go with me.

My concern is that her reticence means she intends to stay an even longer time in Maine. (Of course, I do not know this.) I would like to ask her about this during our call this weekend, but my questions tend to generate tension.

I would also like to ask her about increasing our communication to include daily calls for brief social visits and prayer. We could commit to talk about serious topics only during our scheduled calls with third parties.

I know that there is some pressure around that. Please consider these thoughts and let me know what you think. If you and I could have 10-15 minutes before Suzanne calls so that I can hear your wisdom and pray, that would be a real bonus.

God bless you, and thanks again.

Jim

I said that I knew there was pressure, and indeed there was. People who loved Suzanne very much were concerned about committed time together so soon. Concern was also voiced that being together again in the same place after six months apart would create a honeymoon environment that could cloud judgment.

As the time ticked by from Tuesday until Saturday, I worked and prayed to prepare myself for the call. I wanted to handle myself properly and to let Pastor Wilkerson lead the conversation. The call was scheduled for 10:30 a.m. on August 5, after a deacons' meeting. The meeting went long.

As I stood outside of his office, I watched the hands on a nearby clock rotate slowly and steadily toward and eventually past 10:30. This call was the big moment of my week. It was the time to which I had looked forward in hopes of addressing my fears. Moment by moment the hour grew later. With each tick of the clock, my pulse seemed to quicken. Close to 11:00 a.m., my phone rang, and I saw "Unknown Caller" on the display.

I answered the phone and heard Suzanne's voice. She wondered if she had the wrong time and did not know why Pastor was not answering. I was standing in an all-too-public hallway, so I began walking toward my car as we talked. I explained that the deacons' meeting had gone long and that I had no idea when he would be free. My wife suggested that we talk casually and avoid any deep conversation. This request was wise, and I agreed.

I sat in my car, and in the course of the call, I mentioned again that I was looking forward to November 3.

"Why do you keep referencing that date? You've spoken about it for weeks."

"Of course I have," I answered. "That's the date you said you would drop the protection order."

Uh-oh. I had unwittingly said the wrong words. For the first time in more than three months, the two of us were talking on the phone without a third party present, and my words started a firestorm. Suzanne was floored that I would even make such an assumption. She declared that she had never stated any such intention. The call grew tense, and then she said, "The pastor is calling. Hold on."

Suzanne came back on line to say, "Pastor is in his office and has asked if you could go there to continue the call."

I immediately agreed and sprinted to his office. I arrived and told him all about it with great intensity. Thank God for Pastor Wilkerson.

To me, the idea that Suzanne and I had no timetable was earth-shaking. The light at the end of my lonely tunnel had become the proverbial freight train. To Suzanne, the strength of my response took the reconciliation process back to the beginning. She had thought we were making progress, but now she no longer believed it. Though Pastor helped us recover somewhat, the call in the parking lot was clearly a step backward.

Toward the end of the call, we discussed the coming schedule. Most of her extended family was going to be in town. They had planned some important times together, and Suzanne's extended absences for phone calls would not be a good idea. Furthermore, an anniversary celebration which would be important for the whole family had been planned. Our normal call schedule would not be possible in the coming days.

At that time, my knowledge of Suzanne's life was very limited, but both friends and family had a similar view. Many of those closest to my wife were very concerned about the speed at which we were going. Some thought that she was under pressure to back off; others thought she was under pressure to stay in Maine. I was hearing conflicting reports about how long folks wanted her to stay, but every one of the reports I heard was longer than I had hoped.

The illusion of control fought for a place in my life. Suzanne had purposely chosen the loved ones whose influence she wanted in her life. Because she had purposely chosen to take a break from my daily influence, my mind struggled in unfortunate ways against the reality of the time. The perfect peace derived from a mind stayed on the Father was just out of reach. Fear turned to torment.

On August 9, I contacted several people and simply asked them to pray that God would be move for me as He had in the life of Mordecai and Esther of old. The gallows that had been raised to kill Mordecai had been the instrument of his deliverance. Seemingly much was working against our reconciliation; at the same time, I was growing certain that our separation should draw to a close.

Two days later, at the Men's Advance hosted by the Sauk Trail Baptist Temple in Richton Park, Illinois, I saw one of Suzanne's favorite preachers, Paul Chappell. I approached him, gave him the very basics of my situation, and asked him to pray for us. He agreed.

This meeting, along with the Wednesday evening Bible studies at my church in August, looked as though they would lead to the third transformational change in my spiritual life. But before that transformation had a chance to complete, I would receive a shocking phone call.

On Saturday morning, August 12, Suzanne called me at the pastor's office. As we met to discuss the call, I again prayed, as I had done continually for three days, that God would be the God of Esther for me. The phone rang. We prayed together with the Pastor, and Suzanne asked if she could begin the conversation.

She started by thanking me for all of the work I had done to seek God's restoration in my life. She told me that she had read her May 3 letter repeatedly and that I had done everything she had asked me to do. The day prior, on August 11, against the wishes of many, she had filed for a modification in the protection order. In fact, the order would be changed enough to allow us to live in the same house.

She went on to say that she was considering going to the courthouse with her car loaded so that she could return to Indiana. "Then we can work on our relationship face to face," she continued. She did not yet know when the court date would be, but she was ready to take the next step.

The floodgates were open! Reconciliation River was a river indeed, and the water was rising. I could not believe my ears. Suzanne had been contemplating this court action before I had ever mentioned Esther to anyone. On Tuesday, August 8, she had journaled:

...Jim has definitely changed a lot. I feel like he is right when he told me that home is now a safe place. Thank You, Jesus, for helping Jim to humble himself and accept help. Thank You for your love and mercy and grace. Thank You, Jesus, for Your lovingkindness. We need You. We love You. We give You the glory. Help us, oh, LORD.

Amen, sister! *For I know that in me (that is, in my flesh,) dwelleth no good thing.* (Romans 7:18). If there is any change in me, that change is Christ. If there is any good in me, it is Christ in me. If there is any hope in me, it *is this mystery: Christ in (me), the hope of glory* (Colossians 1:27). Two of four transforming events had already occurred, and the third was underway.

In his August Bible study series about stewardship, Pastor Wilkerson covered three different parables concerning stewards. In all three, the steward without reward had a wrong and bad opinion of the master. So it was with me. I had often challenged my wife in ways similar to the following: "David numbered the people, and seventy THOUSAND people died. Is my life that cheap?" I had a wrong and a bad opinion of the Master. *He that cometh to God **must** believe that he is, and that he is a rewarder of them that diligently seek him.* (Hebrews 11:5).

On the evening of August 12, after more than four decades in the Christian faith, I finally chose to accept the truth that "Jesus loves me! This I know, for the Bible tells me so." One would think this truth to be as plain as the nose on my face, but no temptation had taken me but such as is common to man. Satan has tempted man from the beginning with false accusations about the character of God. Can you almost hear the hiss as Satan lies to Eve? *For God doth know that in the day ye eat thereof, then your eyes shall be opened, and ye shall be as gods, knowing good and evil.* (Genesis 3:5).

Nothing is as great in the universe as His *great love wherewith he loved us* (Ephesians 2:4). Child of God, rejoice! *How precious also are His thoughts unto (you)! How great is the sum of them! If (you) should count them, they are more in number than the sand* (Psalm 139:17, 18).

As mortals, do we not measure outcomes in time? The God of all mercy is eternal. Time is a tool He has entrusted to us that we might measure our days and order our lives. Time is neither His barrier nor His challenge. A day with the LORD is as a thousand years and a thousand years as a day. He is loving and kind. He is just and merciful. We can rest fully assured that *our light affliction, which is but for a moment, worketh for us a far more exceeding and eternal weight of glory*! (II Corinthians 4:17)

God is love; the Bible says so clearly, but understanding and accepting that fact on a personal level is a prerequisite to a working faith. Perfect love casts out fear. It reminds the redeemed that we have a faithful High Priest Who was touched with the feeling of our infirmities that He might invite us to boldly approach the throne of grace to obtain mercy and find grace to help in time of need. In the time of your need, you must know that He loves YOU. He is your FATHER.

The fasting mode was completely over, though for the sake of convenience, I still kept to the same basic diet. I did indulge in a piece of chocolate every night, and I did add spices and bacon drippings to my food. I was also beginning to invite people over on Sunday evenings to see the house. Nearly every room had changes, and I had big expectations that my bride would be home soon. We still had plenty of reasons for caution, but I felt certain that we would spend the week in Colorado Springs together and that we would be together for the holidays. However, setting one's heart on such plans should be done with caution.

The following weekend our church hosted its annual summer marriage seminar. When I learned that the guest speaker would be Clint Caviness, the author of *When Risqué Is Okay*, I thought, *Just what a man three and a half months into loneliness needs—a pep talk on hot sex!* I decided against it, and then for it, and then against it. Eventually my Sunday school teacher, Mark, arranged for me to go for half-price since I would be alone. I went.

Mr. Caviness did not speak about hot sex, but he did speak directly to couples, and the event became a very emotional one for me. Suzanne and I were definitely progressing toward reconciliation, but few feelings are as awkward as being the one single guy in the midst of hundreds of couples. I cannot list one point he spoke about, but I do remember coming to a very clear realization on that Saturday morning that home was now a safe place. I knew it was, and I knew it was time for Suzanne to come home. She would not come to that conclusion as quickly.

HOPEFUL HELPS

- Embrace the love of God!
- Communicate clearly and compassionately.
- The healing process must focus on the needs of the victim.
- God works amazing works.
- Beware of pride.

Embracing Conflict

One of the best preparatory steps for my dreams of reunification had actually started at the end of July. Two days after the seminar was to end, Mom had agreed to come see me. She arrived on August 22. Though my mother had been through horrific health problems in the previous six years, the two of us had made big plans. We planned to take in a baseball game, see "Shakespeare in the Park" (Mom's doctoral dissertation had addressed the role of religion in the way the Bard's writings portrayed women), and enjoy other such delights.

Mom has never lost her sense of fun, and her naturally silver hair in August was now a light shade of purple. I had a rather full, silver beard, so on the way to pick her up at the airport, I stopped at Walgreens and grabbed a can of spray-on purple hair dye. I arrived at Midway early and slipped into the men's room in time to spray my very short hair and longish beard bright purple. We were set to have a BLAST!

My mother's energy levels did not allow for all of our adventures, but ours was a fantastic trip. When a person's life is in disarray and he is down, who in the world is better suited to pick him up than Mom? My mother and I also had some points of contention. Mom had been through two divorces, one of which had stung her particularly hard. Her views of my legal challenges with Suzanne and especially her views of any financial arrangements or potential divorce strongly favored Suzanne. To make life just a bit more spicy, I am far to the right politically, and Mom leans so far to the left that we almost meet each other at our extremities.

In spite of the differences, her visit was magical. Having someone I loved living in my house may have been the best thing that had happened in nearly four months. Conflict, though, was almost immediate. When topics like the court-ordered financial arrangement came up, I felt monstrously betrayed to hear my own mother support Suzanne's position with GREAT fervor. My responses were emotional, and they charged the conflict even more.

As odd as it would seem for a fifty-two-year-old man and his mother, our political differences also provided some spark. These animated conversations were an absolute gift from God. They prepared me to meet a woman with whom I had great conflict and with whom I wanted to create a brand-new marriage. In some ways Suzanne and I were becoming nearly perfect strangers. We had both changed in enormous ways, and we truly did not know each other. My disagreements with Mom became a six-day lesson in how to disagree respectfully.

As you read, may I ask you of yourself? Can you disagree respectfully? Do you have love that does not vaunt itself and is not puffed up? Do you have love that refuses to behave itself unseemly? If you believe you do, have you tested it lately? Can you teach another what it means? Mom and I taught each other.

Late in her visit, which included more wonderful times than I can count and a lot of food without beans or quinoa, I asked my mother a question that made some of the conflicts helpful to her. I asked her if she realized that, as Christians, one of our jobs was to provoke each other to love and good works. We had a responsibility, in good ways, to provoke each other. As much help as I received, this tidbit made some of the conflict helpful to Mom as well.

Suzanne and I were starting to move slowly from the stage of recovering from abuse to the stage of preparing for marriage. Conflict resolution is a key component, and I began to have a fresh appreciation for Chapter 6 in *The Case of the Hopeless Marriage* by Jay Adams. In that very short chapter, Mr. Adams introduces the idea of the "counsel table" (Adams, 2007) as a tool for, among other things, conflict resolution. Chapter 6 is worth the price of the book. I had no idea how weak I was emotionally, so a workable conflict-resolution plan was something I desperately needed. If Pastor Bob had done nothing else for me (and he had done much), his act of introducing me to that book was transformational.

My calls with Suzanne were becoming more and more normal. The edge of formality was being replaced by genuine, heartfelt communication. The work that we had needed to do for decades was well under way. Reconciliation River was flowing swiftly, and soon we would find that fast-flowing rivers are dotted with white water which must be navigated with care, though seemingly, we were more and more up to the challenge.

My journal entry covering August 27 expressed it well:

What a blessed weekend!

On Saturday Suzanne and I had an awesome call with Pastor Wilkerson. We began working on what we need to change for reunification. I am married to a very godly, wise woman! The call went a little sideways on the topic of tithing on the support money I had sent. It had stemmed from the left-over emotional damage inflicted during the original May 26 court date.

I had lunch with McCoys. Their cocker spaniel pup was all over me, but it was a real treat. Thank God for God's wonderful people! On the way there, I had a short, but very sweet, call from Suzanne. Remember the call about tithing, I apologized for not forgiving her after court, and I explained my expectations versus what happened.

Monday, August 28, was a very encouraging day. Suzanne called me at work (while I was in a meeting with HR & Legal) to tell me she loved me. A bit later she called me to ask if we could go through a counseling book together. In a third call we discussed the counseling book and prayed. It was my favorite day since April!

That evening I explained my situation more thoroughly to a pastor who had preached at the "Men's Advance" a few days earlier. My emailed update said:

Good evening.

I am Jim Maxwell, and I asked you to pray for our family at the Men's Advance.

I thought you might enjoy an update.

The very day that I asked you to pray, I had a call with my wife and Pastor Wilkerson. Suzanne had gone to court to drop almost all of the protection order. (I went on to explain the changes to the order.)

Since then we have had increasingly blessed, frequent, and productive calls.

We are now praying and fasting together on Mondays, and last night we added a counseling workbook for another half hour on Mondays. We have regular calls Tuesdays and on the weekends with Brother John, but she is now calling me nearly every day.

On 11/13 we will begin 5 days of intense counseling with these folks (https://caringfortheheart.com), and God is blessing.

If I am still on your prayer list, please thank the LORD on our behalf, and we would consider it a blessing if you would continue to pray.

God bless you,

Jim Maxwell

In a letter that night to the pastor, I added some more detail.

Good evening.

I'm using email because it's late at night, and I don't want to text to bother you.

Suzanne and I had the tithe discussion tonight. We both heard some things we didn't want to hear, but I think I conducted myself with grace.

I believe that God is doing good things, though some of what she heard tonight was hard for her to hear.

Looking forward to more progress soon. I thought it was important to update you.

God bless you,

Jim

After thirty years of marriage, we were finally beginning to grow a Christian marriage. It was as though we were twenty-somethings all over again preparing for marriage. Prayer and fasting, counseling courses, and graceful discussions are supposed to be the normal course in the lives of Christian couples. Are those natural matters of course in your relationships? If not, please do not wait as I did.

For nearly four months I had worked with four counselors per week. I had spent between one and three hours per day alone with God. I had read life-challenging books as a camel drinks water. I had separated myself to God, and I felt as though He was blessing me. I also felt as though the day of our reunion was drawing close. On September 2, Suzanne shocked me with just how close that day might be. I wrote to my coach:

Chris,

In a lengthy counseling session today with Brother John, Suzanne suggested that she might go to the courthouse on September 15 with her bags packed for her return home.

I don't know that that will happen, but things are changing rapidly.

I need the Holy Spirit. I can't get this wrong. I know that in me, that is in my flesh, dwelleth no good thing.

I don't know how well you remember Psalm 38, but it's a Psalm of remembrance which describes my heart very well tonight...

Psalm 38

O LORD, rebuke me not in thy wrath: neither chasten me in thy hot displeasure. For thine arrows stick fast in me, and thy hand presseth me sore. There is no soundness in my flesh because of thine anger; neither is there any rest in my bones because of my sin. For mine iniquities are gone over mine head: as an heavy burden they are too heavy for me.

My wounds stink and are corrupt because of my foolishness. I am troubled; I am bowed down greatly; I go mourning all the day long. For my loins are filled with a loathsome disease: and there is no soundness in my flesh. I am feeble and sore broken: I have roared by reason of the disquietness of my heart.

LORD, all my desire is before thee; and my groaning is not hid from thee. My heart panteth, my strength faileth me: as for the light of mine eyes, it also is gone from me. My lovers and my friends stand aloof from my sore; and my kinsmen stand afar off. They also that seek after my life lay snares for me: and they that seek my hurt speak mischievous things, and imagine deceits all the day long.

But I, as a deaf man, heard not; and I was as a dumb man that openeth not his mouth. Thus I was as a man that heareth not, and in whose mouth are no reproofs. For in thee, O LORD, do I hope: thou wilt hear, O LORD my God. For I said, Hear me, lest otherwise they should rejoice over me: when my foot slippeth, they magnify themselves against me. For I am ready to halt, and my sorrow is continually before me.

For I will declare mine iniquity; I will be sorry for my sin. But mine enemies are lively, and they are strong: and they that hate me wrongfully are multiplied. They also that render evil for good are mine adversaries; because I follow the thing that good is.

Forsake me not, O LORD: O my God, be not far from me. Make haste to help me, O LORD my salvation.

HOPEFUL HELPS

- Seek God.
- Trust God.
- Learn to disagree with grace.
- Learn to disagree with respect.
- Learn the "Counsel Table" method and use it.
- Beware of pride.

Facing Fantasies

Because my wife and I knew the court date would be September 15, we were looking forward to our time in Colorado Springs. Our hearts were learning to trust each other, and in differing ways, we were beginning to anticipate our reunion. I sought to make sure my transformation was real, lasting, and a product of faith. Suzanne, through separate means and methods, did the same. We did not know the details, but we knew that something very real was happening. Even so, yet another major metamorphosis was to come that was a fresh new spring to feed Reconciliation River just prior to our launch.

In early September, as it seemed that the days of our separation were to draw to an end, I found myself in a struggle against anger yet again. I KNEW that this pattern could not exist if Suzanne was at home. I also knew that God had changed me, but there it was—anger. Cognitive dissonance reared its ugly head again; transformation was real, but I was struggling with anger.

I rarely take a lunch at work, but that day I took an early lunch. Around 10:30 in the morning, I abruptly locked my computer, walked away from my desk, and headed outside. As I walked through the Chicago Loop, I found myself on the River Walk, mulling over a conversation several weeks prior with my coach, Chris Moles. I did not document the conversation well, but as I recall, Chris had asked to me to describe what it was like for me when anger arose. I answered him something like this: "In your mind, go to your front door. Open the door and look down. See a rattlesnake. You KNOW that it is bad. You know that it is dangerous. It is a threat to your family. If it strikes, it could change everything for everyone you love. Feel the fear; feel the adrenaline; feel the anger. You must attack that snake. You KNOW you must kill the snake. Now, erase the snake, but keep all of the feelings."

I went on to say that the longer a conflict persisted, the more words I said, and the more I thought on the topic at hand, the more intense the feelings would grow. Chris and I discussed the April 14 letter and the way that my outrageous response to it had eventually led to Suzanne's decision to separate. He asked where the rattlesnake came from on April 14. I explained that the snake had come from Suzanne's motives and intentions in omitting me from the letter. Chris admonished me that God wants us to feel emotion. He actually commands it. He asked me to read from Philippians 4.

Rejoice in the LORD alway: and again I say, Rejoice. Let your moderation be known unto all men. The LORD is at hand. Be careful for nothing; but in everything by prayer and supplication with thanksgiving let your requests be made known unto God. And the peace of God, which passeth all understanding, shall keep your hearts and minds through Christ Jesus. Finally, brethren, whatsoever things are true, whatsoever things are honest, whatsoever things are just, whatsoever things are pure, whatsoever things are lovely, whatsoever things are of good report; if there be any virtue, and if there be any praise, think on these things.

After some further teaching and admonition, Chris asked me how often others were accurate when they told me my motives or when they explained to me what I was thinking. I replied that people were almost never right in such situations. He then asked how likely it was that my determination about Suzanne's motives or intentions were true. I agreed that it was not likely. "If they were not true," he queried, "is it honest of you to judge or condemn her for them?" Of course it was not. Chris went down the line, "If it was not true or honest, was my anger just, pure, or lovely? Was it of good report? Was it virtuous? Was it praiseworthy?" The man should have been a prosecuting attorney.

As I walked along the banks of the Chicago River on that beautiful day, mulling over the conversation, I looked up II Corinthians 10 on my phone and took in verses 3-5:

For though we walk in the flesh, we do not war after the flesh: (for the weapons of our warfare are not carnal, but mighty through God to the pulling down of strong holds;) casting down imaginations, and every high thing that exalteth itself against the knowledge of God, and bringing into captivity every thought to the obedience of Christ

I looked at the definition of *imaginations* from the *Strong's Hebrew and Greek Lexicons*© (Public Domain) on my phone app. The Greek word was *logimós*. The definition included the following:

1. a reckoning, computation
2. a reasoning; such as is hostile to the Christian faith
3. a judgment, decision; such as conscience passes

What was a reckoning or computation that was also a high thing exalting itself against the knowledge of God? Verse 7 asked the question, *Do ye look on things after the outward appearance?* Paul was talking about the carnal Christians in Corinth who questioned his authority as an apostle. That thought drew my mind to similar words.

In I Samuel 16:7 God had contrasted Jesse's eldest, Eliab, with David, using these words: *But the LORD said unto Samuel, Look not on his countenance, or on the height of his stature; because I have refused him: for the LORD seeth not as man seeth; for man looketh on the outward appearance, but the LORD looketh on the heart.* From Genesis 6:5, where God saw that the imaginations and thoughts of human hearts were evil, to the Gospels, where Christ knew the thoughts of the Pharisees, it seemed more and more to me that the thoughts of another person's heart were indeed God's domain.

God knows the future; I do not. God knows the absolute truth about the present; I do not. God knows every thought in every head and every heart of every person; I get confused with my own thoughts. When I listen to Suzanne and decide, or dare I say judge, her motives, is that a reckoning or computation that exalts itself against the knowledge of God? Is that part of what it means to idolatrously enter His domain?

Somewhere near Michigan Avenue, I turned and began retracing my steps back to the office. The beauty of the river was but a blur in the background. Much of what had made my technical career successful was my ability to quickly assess technical problems. Upon learning just a few technical details, I had frequently found quick success in solving problems others had struggled with. At work I had successfully taken incomplete knowledge and filled in unknown facts with my assumptions.

Suzanne is not a computer; neither are you. Compared to you, computers are temporal and slow. People are eternal beings with bodies, souls, spirits, and minds. Your mind is more complex than most computer networks of today, and your social, spiritual, and family networks are vastly more complex. If you are a Christian, the Holy Spirit of God inhabits your spirit. Yes, your mind is God's domain. No person can fathom you, solve you, or judge you. Any attempt to do so is pure imagination.

The words began to echo more and more loudly in my head:

...the weapons of our warfare are not carnal, but mighty through God to the pulling down of strong holds;) casting down imaginations, and every

high thing that exalteth itself against the knowledge of God, and bringing into captivity every thought to the obedience of Christ (II Corinthians 10:4, 5).

I began to realize that for my thoughts to be obedient to Christ, I had to abandon God's domain and trust Him to manage it. I could not superimpose my imaginary thoughts over the reality of what another was thinking. Suzanne's thoughts and motives belonged to her. Only she and God were privy to her thoughts or motives unless or until she shared them.

The phone rang, and the Caller ID said "Unknown Caller." I knew it was my wife, and I answered with a swirling flurry of words. This change was transformational. I did not have all of the words down, and I am sure that some of my thoughts were incoherent. I do not remember why she called, but we talked about imaginations. She opened her Bible, and we read together.

Truth can be exciting, especially that type of truth that sets you free. As the graceful waters of Reconciliation rose around us, my wife and I could both see the patterns of our past! Sinful habits which have grown in a heart for decades can grow very deep roots. Roots such as these are strongholds. *But the weapons of our warfare are mighty to the pulling down of such strongholds*, and the bastion of imagination was starting to topple in my life.

Putting the spiritual rest of the Christian mind into perspective is hard. While the Holy Spirit certainly is a "Higher Power," He is much more than that. The eternal God indwells the body of the believer, but He does not impose Himself. He accepts what we give and gives it back blessed. Consider the second chapter of I Corinthians:

And I, brethren, when I came to you, came not with excellency of speech or of wisdom, declaring unto you the testimony of God. For I determined not to know any thing among you, save Jesus Christ, and him crucified. And I was with you in weakness, and in fear, and in much trembling.

And my speech and my preaching was not with enticing words of man's wisdom, but in demonstration of the Spirit and of power: that your faith should not stand in the wisdom of men, but in the power of God. Howbeit we speak wisdom among them that are perfect: yet not the wisdom of this world, nor of the princes of this world, that come to nought: but we speak the wisdom of God in a mystery, even the hidden wisdom, which God

ordained before the world unto our glory: which none of the princes of this
world knew: for had they known it, they would not have crucified the LORD
of glory.

But as it is written, Eye hath not seen, nor ear heard, neither have
entered into the heart of man, the things which God hath prepared for
them that love him. But God hath revealed them unto us by his Spirit: for
the Spirit searcheth all things, yea, the deep things of God. For what man
knoweth the things of a man, save the spirit of man which is in him? even
so the things of God knoweth no man, but the Spirit of God. Now we have
received, not the spirit of the world, but the spirit which is of God; that we
might know the things that are freely given to us of God. Which things also
we speak, not in the words which man's wisdom teacheth, but which the
Holy Ghost teacheth; comparing spiritual things with spiritual.

But the natural man receiveth not the things of the Spirit of God: for
they are foolishness unto him: neither can he know them, because they are
spiritually discerned. But he that is spiritual judgeth all things, yet he
himself is judged of no man. For who hath known the mind of the LORD,
that he may instruct him? but we have the mind of Christ.

Overstating the difference between the mental machinations of human
coping mechanisms and the spiritual help of surrendering one's mind to
the Holy Spirit is impossible. The LORD describes it in Romans 6:12-14:

Let not sin therefore reign in your mortal body, that ye should obey it
in the lusts thereof. Neither yield ye your members as instruments of
unrighteousness unto sin: but yield yourselves unto God, as those that are
alive from the dead, and your members as instruments of righteousness
unto God. For sin shall not have dominion over you: for ye are not under
the law, but under grace.

Without question, the brain is the most significant member of the body,
but my brain is still a member—a body part. As I yield my eyes to Him to
look upon that which He would have me see, or as I yield my feet to Him
to go where He would have me go, I yield my mind and seek His grace for
help with those sins which originate in my mind—all of them.

HOPEFUL HELPS

- Tear down the stronghold of imaginations and every high thing
  that exalts itself against the knowledge of God.
- Beware of pride.

Making Out

In the end, Suzanne chose to leave on Monday, September 18, to come home. She made the journey into a delightful road trip with her mother, tracing my mother-in-law's roots through several states. They had a refreshing time and enjoyed the company of relatives. Theirs was the type of mother/daughter trip every mother and daughter should take.

On Wednesday night, September 20, Suzanne texted to let me know her schedule. She and her mother would eat at Chick-fil-A in Merrillville and then would head to Mark and Missy's house. She would spend Wednesday night, Thursday night, and Friday night with our friends, and she would be back in our house after the renewal of vows on Saturday. They would arrive while I was at church.

I wanted to leave and meet them at the restaurant, but Suzanne insisted that she needed to get to Missy's house and have a few minutes to freshen up first. I sat in the very last pew of the church in the aisle seat nearest the door nearest the car with the car pointed toward Schererville. As the congregation stood to sing the closing hymn, I bolted for the car and very nearly crossed the sound barrier on my way to the car. I obeyed every traffic law—no room for a ticket on this trip! At about 9:00 p.m., we met.

It was a fast, frightful, delightful, and very busy few days.

Just a few weeks prior, loved ones had been concerned that if we reunited for the first time during our counseling session in Colorado, the session might be skewed by an inevitable honeymoon period. That assessment may have been the most accurate warning anyone had given us. When we met again for the first time in person, it was awkward and stilted, but within moments, both of our hearts turned to water.

I asked Suzanne if we could take a short walk. As we stepped out of Missy's house, I took her hand, and we strolled down a dark, sparsely lit road, chirping like lovebirds. At a gravel cul-de-sac, we stepped into the shadows. September 20 was a new moon, but in the light cast by nearby houses, I gazed into her eyes and leaned forward to kiss my wife. Our lips melted together, and we cuddled close in the softest, warmest embrace of my life. Short, sweet kisses were interspersed with long, deep, passionate kisses.

We had chosen to renew our wedding vows on Saturday, September 23.

Until that time we would not live together as a married couple, and in the cool breezes of that late summer night, I promised her the gift of restraint. I made promises about how far we would NOT go in our romantic touching until after the renewal. Nevertheless, the kissing continued until we were embarrassed at the length of our absence.

We walked back hand-in-hand, talking about the thrill of our future, the fun of her trip, and the goodness of our God. As we found a final dark shadow in our friends' driveway, we made out again, albeit much more briefly. Then we parted.

These rekindled affections intensified over the next couple of days. Suzanne and I dropped my mother-in-law off at Midway Airport on Friday morning, and we spent the rest of the day alone together. Most of the day was spent at our house, preparing for the renewal. Having Anne Murray singing "Could I Have This Dance" in the background did not hurt matters, but we frequently stopped working to look into each other's eyes and kiss. Kiss we did, and these kisses were deeper, tenderer, softer, and more meaningful than any kisses I had ever imagined. Something was very intense and yet tranquil about each caress. Words are but a paltry attempt to describe it.

My purpose here is not turn a book about spiritual hope into a romance novella, nor is it to embarrass my modest wife. The point is this: PASSION IS REAL, and two hearts separated by time will not come back together free from its effects. The heart can at times be much more powerful than the mind. Love songs may declare that it is pure or simple for something to come from the heart rather than from the head, but passion is neither entirely pure nor acceptably simple. It has the power to overpower. Premature reunification carries this risk.

Where there has been abuse, there must be transformation. A metamorphosis must prepare the way of peace. I thank the LORD that time has shown Suzanne and has confirmed to me that we were ready, but I must confess that neither of us had understood the dangers of passion in reuniting prematurely.

When determining the timing of reunification, one must understand what can happen on dates or times alone. God's proper order for making important decisions is spirit, soul, and body. God's Holy Spirit is to work with the spirit of man to inform the soul on how to rule the body. The body may at times demand that the soul ignore the spirit and give way to passion. Thinking in terms of the strife that lives in an abusive relationship, consider the admonition of James 3:13-18.

Who is a wise man and endued with knowledge among you? let him shew out of a good conversation his works with meekness of wisdom. But if ye have bitter envying and strife in your hearts, glory not, and lie not against the truth. This wisdom descendeth not from above, but is earthly, sensual, devilish. For where envying and strife is, there is confusion and every evil work.

But the wisdom that is from above is first pure, then peaceable, gentle, and easy to be intreated, full of mercy and good fruits, without partiality, and without hypocrisy. And the fruit of righteousness is sown in peace of them that make peace.

Where abuse has occurred, the safety and wellbeing of the victim is the beginning, heart, and end of every process. Caution is more than a watchword; it is a vital safeguard. Counseling and guidance should not wane during any transition period. Passion has its place, and that place is at the righteous end of godly peace.

Suzanne and I did have some safeguards in place, and these are good procedures to be encouraged by wise counselors. We established a framework of people to help us with accountability. There were people, whose names I did not know, who were to act on Suzanne's behalf if she did not check in daily with a good report. I had people to whom I gave account on a daily basis. They had agreed to hear Suzanne, and she was prepared to be open and honest.

HOPEFUL HELPS

- Beware of passion, premature reunions, or time alone, which can be dangerous.
- Beware of pride.

Living Happily

Happily ever after makes for a nice ending, but life after separation is not an ending. It is a beginning. Our beginning was bumpy. After the renewal, we had decided that we wanted to honor the Lord in our beginnings, so the first thing we did was to make a soul-winning visit. We then went home and stayed over for Sunday at our church. When the morning service was finished, we left for a three-day honeymoon in Michigan.

If honeymoons predicted marriages, then we were in trouble. What we didn't know about the transition was that we were BOTH completely different people. Suzanne had lived in freedom for months, with support and love. She had goals for the type of woman she would be and for the type of life we would live together.

I had lived in virtual isolation with a strange life. Up before every alarm and alone for hours on end, I had endlessly pursued everything I could find on the path to God. There had been perfect freedom in my schedule, diet, and sleep patterns. I, too, had pictures of how our new marriage would be. One factor was impossible to prepare for; we were each bound by the vows of marriage to a near perfect stranger. There was hope, but work was needed.

The biblical roles in our marriage had been reversed, as Suzanne had stood for righteousness and had required proof of change before we were to come back together. She had set the conditions for every conversation and for the reunion itself. Knowing that we had not lived as partners, I asked her to write our first budget while were on that honeymoon. The trust needed for progress was trust that had to be rebuilt slowly.

A little more than a month after the renewal, we made the anticipated trip to Colorado Springs for a week of counseling. It was arduous work, and it left both of us emotionally exhausted at the end of every day. We spent the afternoons at the Garden of the Gods or at the Navigators' Castle. We walked and talked and did our counseling homework. We also played Ping Pong™, and Suzanne established her yet-to-be-challenged dominance at the Ping Pong™ table.

The counseling focused not only on the hurts in our marriage, but the hurts we had both brought into our marriage. Our counselor gave us personality tests. We each completed our own profile. Then we completed profiles on each other. We learned lessons on caring for each other according to knowledge. God seemed to give us illustrations for our lessons. It was a beautiful, prosperous week.

We established weekly counseling sessions with our home pastor, and I continued weekly meetings with my psychologist, as well as one other pastor. We each had an "accountability partner" to monitor our new home for signs of abuse. Happily ever after was the journey we wanted to take, but the first steps were rough. Suzanne had been hurt through the years, and her amazing spirit of forgiveness has preserved so much.   As I continue to live with her, I believe Suzanne is a living example of Jesus' admonition to Peter in Matthew 18:21-22. *Then came Peter to him, and said, Lord, how oft shall my brother sin against me, and I forgive him? till seven times? Jesus saith unto him, I say not unto thee, Until seven times: but, Until seventy times seven.* Unfortunately, not all relationships in our lives had been blessed with the same resilience.

Thirty years of abuse creates a lot of wounds. Some wounds become scars, and some heal. Other wounds stay open and fester. I cannot require anyone to forgive me. Perhaps some never will.

The tragic truth is that my wife must now live with the consequences of the hurts I inflicted on others. This book has focused on the restoration of one relationship, but we neither live to ourselves nor die to ourselves. If we were to give thirty years to fix those things that took thirty years to break, it might not be enough. Moreover, we have no promise that we will even live another thirty years.

Our little household is the only place we could start. From Colorado Springs, to the office of Pastor Wilkerson, to the books we have read and the marriage retreats we have attended, God has blessed us. *Where sin abounded, grace did much more abound.* (Romans 5:28b)

Jay Adams' "Counsel Table" was an amazing help, especially in the earliest days of our new marriage. We also learned to lean greatly upon prayer. We redecorated our guest room, with the help of Suzanne's mother, and named it the Prayer Room. Nearly every time we came to an impasse of any kind, we would go together to the Prayer Room, pull out our big pillows, and kneel before our Father seeking His help. Prayer is pivotal, and we continue this tradition today.

In the course of time, our counseling sessions became fewer and less frequent. In time we learned to love and be loved in new ways—better ways. We seem to find new plateaus on a regular basis where we look at each other and admit that we never knew that marriage could be this good.

We still have conflict. We still have counselors. We still have need for growth, but our lives have been transformed.

In reality, happily-ever-after is in the realm of our Father. And we, *being predestinated according to the purpose of him who worketh all things after the counsel of his own will: that we should be to the praise of his glory* (Ephesians 1:11b-12a) are truly on the journey to happily-ever-after. Our futures are bright because *we know that all things work together for good to them that love God, to them who are the called according to his purpose. For whom he did foreknow, he also did predestinate to be conformed to the image of his Son, that he might be the firstborn among many brethren.* (Romans 8:28-29)

We thank God for His transforming power and amazing grace. Our lives are richly, wonderfully blessed. We love our new lives, and we desperately want to share His grace with others. To that end, we wrote this book. To that end, we continue to read books appropriate to helping victims and perpetrators of abuse, and to that same end we have enrolled in Chris Moles' PeaceWorks University (PWU).

PWU has provided a place where we work weekly to learn more about advocacy in the area of domestic abuse, and it is a community of believers dedicated to that same cause. It has grown in scope and membership. It has introduced us to other training opportunities, and it has introduced us to likeminded Christians who have been wonderfully encouraging as we seek to minister to those hurt by sins similar to mine.

God has already brought many abuse victims across our path. It has been our privilege to advocate for some wonderful ladies, and we have had the opportunity to encourage some who, like me, have lived hurtful lives at home. We have begun to reach out to pastors of churches in our area to alert them to the problems in their own pews, and to this point, we have been well received. It has been our privilege to share our testimony in public venues and private conversations.

Suzanne is compiling a booklet of her own essays. We hope to publish it soon. Victims are powerful advocates, and her testimony is moving. She works tirelessly to help those she can help, and she encourages me. She always was the wife of my dreams. She is a loving sweetheart; she is a godly partner; she is a diligent homemaker; she is a fun-loving buddy; she is a tender lover; she is a faithful friend.

With those thoughts in mind, here is a note from Suzanne.

Psalms 9:9 says, *The LORD also will be a refuge for the oppressed, a refuge in times of trouble.* **And Isaiah 1:17 says,** *Learn to do well; seek judgment, <u>relieve the oppressed</u>, judge the fatherless, plead for the widow.*

Our pastor is still our counselor. One day we decided to take him a coffee to his office. When we realized he had someone in the office with him, we began to apologize for interrupting. He quickly explained that one of these two ladies (we will call her Edna) was in his office because her husband was abusing her, and she was afraid to go home. The other lady (we will call her Holly) was a widow and a long-time friend of the abuse victim. Holly was helping Edna to explain to the pastor what was really going on at Edna's home. Pastor asked if we would be willing to help. We sat down with the pastor and these two precious ladies, and our journey of helping the oppressed continued in earnest.

We helped to find Edna a safe place to live. We helped her get to counsel. We helped her get a protection order from the courts. There are many things you can do to help victims! We enjoyed watching God provide for Edna's every need. Edna had a full-time job, but now, she had no car. Two other ladies from our church agreed to help me get her to and from work each day. For over two months we did this, and then one day a special event took place!

Holly was walking, as she so often did, and the owner of a nearby body shop (the shop owner, a Christian man who attends a church in our area, who we will call Jason) stopped and offered her a FREE CAR! Holly answered him, "I don't drive anymore, but I have a friend who needs a car..." When Holly contacted Edna about the car, we were elated!

When we arrived at the body shop, we spoke with Jason. He asked to hear Edna's story. After he heard her story, we were amazed and delighted to discover that Jason's mother-in-law was a resident where the Edna was working, and, in fact, Edna knew the mother-in-law and had made breakfast for her many times...Wow!

Then Jason told us how he got the car. Over a year ago, he noticed some children playing in the yard near his shop. He went

outside to check on them and found their parents there near a car that had been in an accident. They were from a neighboring state, and they were hoping to get their car fixed. The cost to fix it and the age of the car led them to give the title to the owner rather than fix it up. Jason told them he would fix it up and give the car away to someone in need. During the year that the owner had this car on his lot, a couple of people had come to look at it, but somehow, their stories didn't seem to validate the gift. However, when the owner heard Edna's story, he said, "I know that you are the girl for this car!" Wow…huge answer to prayer! Isn't God good to give us so many blessings!

Our church has been remarkable. I dedicated this book to my brothers and sisters because of the amazing way they brought God's grace to me and to us through our trials and through the process of our reconciliation. Since then we have been blessed by ministry opportunities, marriage retreats, new friends, and constant growth.

We are looking forward to adding content to our website. We want to publish our own testimonies, and we want to publish the helpful, goodly testimonies of others as God gives us opportunity. We also hope to make this book available as an audio book.

I am blessed. We are blessed. Grace abounds. God is faithful. There is hope.

Looking Back

Perhaps, as a reader, you wonder how a woman gets caught in such a trap. Have you asked yourself why Suzanne stayed? Have you asked how she found the courage to leave? Have you wondered why she ever considered coming back? Every case is different, but the following are her words.

Hi, my name is Suzanne, and I grew up in an apple orchard in Maine, helping my father with readying the apples for harvest and milking our goats. In 1980 God brought me to Hyles-Anderson College in Northwest Indiana, located close to the big city of Chicago.

In 1983 a Texan named Jim Maxwell also came to the college, and we met while working on a church bus route. In 1987 we married, and in 1988 we had our first child, a son, and then in 1991 we had our second child, a daughter.

If you had told me when I was a little girl living an idyllic life in an apple orchard and milking goats that I would live near and work in the big city of Chicago, I would have been scared to death! Growing up in my home when I was a child was AMAZING! By the time I was born, my father had accepted a pastorate. I was the second of five kids, with an older brother, two sisters younger than I, and then another brother. There are ten years between my brothers.

My siblings and I grew up in a loving, Christian home. My parents had met at a Christian college, and they both grew up in Christian homes. I had good Christian examples who placed a great emphasis on godly living. My parents lived godly lives in front of my siblings and me.

I grew up attending church Sunday morning, Sunday night, and Wednesday night, and I went to church activities. Really, I was kept very, very, very sheltered and insulated from the influence of the world. My pastor-father was a gentle father and wise leader who was very unassuming, self-sacrificing, and unselfish in everything. He also assisted his mother and his mother's sisters by laboring around their homes to make sure they were cared for and comfortable. He was a very good son and also a good nephew to his aunts.

Mom grew up in a pastor's home in a very large family, and her father also sold Bibles. Much of the responsibilities to care for the many siblings fell upon Mom's shoulders. This was especially true during the time when my grandmother had to care for a child born with the afflictions of spina bifida. My aunt died at the age of just 16 months. My grandparents on both sides of my family were saved and loved the LORD.

I grew up as a fearful child. Little by little God was teaching me to trust Him. It was my heart's desire to do what God wanted me to do with my life. After high school graduation, I asked a pastor who was a graduate of Liberty Baptist College (now Liberty University) where I should go to college, and he said, "Hyles-Anderson College." My older brother had attended Liberty, but because the pastor said Hyles-Anderson was the greatest Christian college in America or in the world, I applied and was accepted.

I had never been farther west than Ohio, so when I left home in the fall of 1980 and flew to Indiana, I was much afraid. I didn't know anybody at the college; however, one of my mom's sisters lived in Chicago. I didn't know her extremely well, but I had been in the same family gathering with her a few times. She picked me up at the airport and gave me a ride to the college.

I would say that during my first year, I lived an extremely fearful life and didn't relax until I had made myself sick. At the end of the first year, I prayed, "LORD, if You want me to be here, I'm not going to do this to myself anymore. I'm not going to be afraid. I'm just going to give my fear to You." As soon I made the decision to give my fear to the LORD, I had peace. The rest of my years at college were free from this type of fear.

I was serving in the "C" church bus ministry, and the leader, Dr. Ray Young, asked me if I would switch routes so that I could be a bus-calling partner with the captain's wife. I did, and in changing bus routes, I met Jim Maxwell, a freshman at the college. Shortly thereafter, he asked me to leave the route so that we could date (The school did not permit excessive dating between workers on the same bus route.), and I answered, "You know what? We just met; let's be friends."

For the first year he was in college, we were friends only, worked on the same bus route, and had the maximum allowable dates, which I believe was two at that time. The following year Jim asked me to leave the route again, and I went to another route in the division so that we could date. Soon we were engaged, and then in 1987, we were married.

As a single young lady in the college, I remember my pastor, Dr. Hyles, often preaching that he grew up in the home of a very godly mother and a drunkard father. He would sometimes disclose how his drunken father would physically abuse his mother and how she would crawl back to him on her hands and knees and wrap her arms around his legs and say, "I love you, Athey, I love you."

From his illustrations, I thought that a good Christian was being submissive to the point of loving an abusive husband and continuing to behave like a good Christian. I honestly thought that tolerating abuse would make my children great because it seemed to have worked that way for my pastor when he grew up in an abusive home.

Jim and I were happily married in Maine, and then on the way home on our honeymoon, Jim lost his temper. Many times thereafter, my husband would become angry and lose his temper. I had grown up in a home where there were no displays of anger and never any abuse. I thought my job was to be a good example of a sweet, submissive, and kind wife—always.

I wasn't always a good example because I wasn't perfect, but I tried to be a good example at all times. Most of the times that I asked Jim to seek counseling, he did not want to go because he did not want me to tattle on him.

I went to my pastor and asked, "If the Bible says 'obey your husbands in all things,' does that mean I cannot seek counsel if my husband says I cannot?" He answered, "Yes."

One time I took evidence of abuse to a family in the church, but I believe they were too afraid to do anything about it or they simply didn't know what to do.

I lived with the abuse for twenty-nine years. Some years were much better than others. Finally, after pleading the blood of Christ over our home, I decided that from that point on, I was going to tell the truth. I was not going to pretend that everything was "okay," and I would seek help regardless of what anyone said. After all, I had done everything I had known to do, and nothing had seemed to work. Always the same problems would creep up and haunt the two of us.

On May 3, 2017, I left Indiana with my dog, Mocha, for Maine to go to a safe place until my husband could get help for the deep issues in his heart that were causing him to lose his temper and respond to me in anger.

While I was in Maine, God did some amazing things in the heart of my husband. Also while I was in Maine, I felt the lovingkindness of the LORD in so many ways. In innumerable ways, God sent me hugs that showed me His great love.

God gave me peace in the midst of the storm, and I had a wonderful summer doing things for family members and spending time with my family. I was also able to have vital peace and rest. After seeking advice, I went to court and obtained a Protection from Abuse Order against my husband, and it was granted for a year. I knew that at any time I could go back to the court and ask for the order to be revised. I could contact him, but he could in no way contact me. I had decided that I would contact him for the first time on our thirtieth wedding anniversary, July 2, 2017.

Our pastor in Indiana, Pastor Wilkerson, started reaching out to me via text messages and phone calls. After Jim and I had our first phone call on our anniversary, Pastor set up times to be on the call with us so that he could determine how the call was going, how our relationship was progressing, and how to be sure no abuse would take place during the phone call. It was so helpful having a capable counselor join our calls! It was vital to the reestablishing of our relationship.

Jim had humbled himself in amazing ways. The first step was going in front of our entire church of thousands of people to confess and acknowledge that he had abusive anger for thirty years in our marriage. I am so glad that our God is a God of forgiveness—a God of love, kindness, and reconciliation. I am glad that our God is a merciful God and that He is always faithful to us.

Jim has offered many ideas in the preceding pages. I have read them, and I am glad that they are in print. Even so, I do have a few thoughts of my own. With sincere hope that my thoughts will be helpful, here are a few:

1) Your philosophy about marriage is vital. Consider Matthew 19:3-12. Believe with all of your heart that God wants your marriage to be for life! Never consider divorce. Life is better when we settle the divorce issue in our hearts before the wedding.

2) Marry a godly Christian. II Corinthians 6:14 says, *Be ye not unequally yoked together with unbelievers.* Life will be better if you and your spouse are both headed in the same direction!

3) Marriage should equal unity. Mark 10:8 says, *And they twain shall be one flesh: so then they are no more twain, but one flesh.* While dating, you and your future husband should have similar spiritual desires. Beware if while dating there is much strife. After you become one flesh, separation or divorce causes a tearing apart of that body. Unity is so much better.

4) Do not date or marry an angry person. Proverbs 22:24-25 instructs us, *Make no friendship with an angry man; and with a furious man thou shalt not go: lest thou learn his ways, and get a snare to thy soul.*

5) Yield to the Lord Jesus Christ and to each other. Yielding takes humility. Jesus humbled himself when He left Heaven and became a man. Christ took upon Himself the form of a servant and was made in the likeness of men. What a great example He was of what we ought to be!

6) FORGIVE 70x7. Peter asked Jesus in Matthew 18:21-22 how many times he should forgive his brother. *Jesus saith unto him, I say not unto thee, until seven times: but, until seventy times seven.* That equals 490 times! That is a lot of forgiveness and patience! It is enduring love. Forgive *every time*, and you will not become bitter. Bitterness grows deep like a root to destroy you and your relationships, but forgiveness will prevent that destruction.

7) Pray much for those who hurt you.

8) Take a stand for righteousness and act early...at the **first sign** of abuse. If you allow abuse, you give your spouse permission to abuse you again. Please do not wait 29 years.

9) God cares about you **and your children**. Protect your children! Psalm 72:4 says, *He shall judge the poor of the people,* **he shall save the children of the needy, and shall break in pieces the oppressor.** God is a God of justice and hates violence. Get help before your children suffer.

10) Get to a safe place! Proverbs 27:12 says, *A prudent man foreseeth the evil, and hideth himself.* Psalm 9:9 says, *The LORD also will be a refuge for the oppressed, a refuge in times of trouble.* Aren't you glad that God cares for his own?!

11) Be discreet. Limit who you tell and what you say. While you are in your safe place, it is best that only a few know your details.

12) Get help! If your church uses the discipline in Matthew 18, seek help there. If necessary, go to court for a protection order.

13) Stay spiritual! Seek godly counsel, including that of a godly pastor and godly women. Read good books. Listen to podcasts. Read your Bible daily, often. (The Psalms were very helpful to me.) Be faithful to church and to prayer. Be a servant.

Stay busy because an idle mind is the Devil's workshop.
JOURNAL EVERYTHING.

14) Stay physically active! Exercise! A healthy body is vital to keeping a healthy mind, and a healthy mind will help you to stay strong. II Timothy 1:7 says, *For God hath not given us the spirit of fear; but of power, and of love, and of a sound mind.*

15) Get emotional help. Find a women's support group and go share with others.

16) Never limit God. Expect a miracle. God specializes in things we think are impossible.

17) KNOW THAT THERE IS HOPE! With God, ALL THINGS ARE POSSIBLE. God comes into our lives, cleans us up, and makes us usable. To God be all of the glory for great things He hath done!

HOPEFUL HELPS

My beloved brothers and sisters, abuse exists in church families. Is it not time to stand and address it? While the problem of abuse is far wider than any single faith, there is no room for it in ours.

Do we need to own our faults and change the way we present ours doctrine? Absolutely! How can we delay to address our issues immediately and thoroughly? We may not be aware of what happens inside of another's home, but by calling sin by its name, we can shine light into the darkness.

The ladies of our churches must know that the church belongs to Christ. May they trust through our example that He loves them and that His body will protect them? Would-be abusers must understand that they will be held accountable for their actions and that actions in the home are subject to the same law of love as any other actions.

There never was a time in a church congregation for chest thumping bravado as a way to address marital abuse. If such a practice has come to a congregation, it must end. There are abusive relationships in nearly every congregation, and in facing that fact, each congregation must protect the abused and redeem the abuser. To fail this mission is to spread the problem. Abusive men can be redeemed through loving strength. The work is grueling and heartrending but worth every drop of sweat or blood. As God's people we can make a difference, and we must.

Wrapping Up

In this text I have attempted to chronicle the steps through which God gently walked me during the early days of my restoration and reconciliation. God's work our lives is relational, not academic. The story covers the time when my relationship with the Lord grew in some necessary ways. In the areas where I grew, He ordered the steps I took.

To the extent I did not articulate the steps well, the following is a synopsis of what I perceive that God has done in my life over the three thousand, four hundred, and twenty-one hours from my confrontation to the my renewal of vows with Suzanne:

Repentance

God gave me a heart that:

- Acknowledged my sins
    - Individually and collectively to the best of my frail, mortal ability
    - In detail for most of the moments of May 5 and May 6
    - In resounding pulses for many weeks and continuing at times through present day
- Shed tears of grief over what I had done and caused (NOTE: This reaction is the polar opposite of the tears shed over what I had lost!)
    - Almost unceasingly on May 5 and May 6
    - Daily and with great frequency for several weeks
    - Publicly and privately with those I had hurt and with those who were helping me
- I apologized to several of Suzanne's friends and one of her ministries. I regret that I did not address the girls in her Sunday school class prior to our reunion. To the best of our abilities, this error has been corrected.
- Also in resounding pulses for many weeks and continuing at times through the present day

Separation and dedication *Through desire a man, having separated himself, seeketh and intermeddleth with all wisdom* (Proverbs 18:1). God gave me a heart, a mind, and a will that were "all-in."

- I started every day spending significant time with God.

- Hebrews 13:7, *Remember them which have the rule over you, who have spoken unto you the word of God: whose faith follow, considering the end of their conversation.* I sought to follow Pastor Wilkerson's faith. His conversation, or manner of living, is humble, godly, prudent, and kind. His faith is worthy of following. He has truly and faithfully spoken to me the Word of God.
- I worked with Chris Moles, and I read his book more than once. *The Heart of Domestic Abuse* and his coaching were and are invaluable. May God give America thousand more just like him!
- I spent countless hours with Pastor Craig. He is faithful first to God, but he has known me for decades and was unflinching in his willingness to kindly rebuke me for bad thinking and to direct me in the ways of wisdom. Craig was a sounding board and confidante who answered back with truth. He is one of the most important friends in my life.
- I counseled with Pastor Bob. He candidly, humbly, and kindly encouraged me toward those ingredients which should be added into a godly marriage, should Suzanne and I ever reconcile.
- I worked with a professional psychotherapist: I do not worship at the altar of secular humanism, but I do recognize the fact that diligent, smart people have studied to understand concepts I do not understand. In a Christian context, I gave diligence to learn from Steve and apply what insights he had into our healing; I did so with gravity and diligence.
- I read constantly, averaging more than a book a week, and sometimes a book a day. I read articles, watched YouTubes, and did homework with the curriculum I received from Chris Moles.
- I met with and learned from people who had seen success where I had failed, including the following:
  - A professional acquaintance who was reconciled to her husband after he was jailed for abusing her
  - A couple who had separated under similar circumstances to ours and who had seen transformation
  - The chairman of our deacon board and his wife, whose life and marriage are worth learning
  - Charlie and Glenda, two godly Christians who reared

wonderful kids in a loving home and whose lights so shine that one may see their good works and glorify their Father which is in Heaven
- Suzanne's friends
- Others who were willing

I made my whole life about becoming what God wanted me to be for Him and for her.

Unless I was with other people, I basically ate only beans, quinoa, fruits, and vegetables. I did not seek pleasure in food—except for blueberries (Pray for me; I may be addicted to plump, beautiful, Michigan blueberries.).

I worked for hours every day to express my love to Suzanne with my hands. Since it was against the law for me to call or write, I installed new floors in four rooms, painted two rooms, built a Ping Pong™ table divider, hung new drapes, tiled the tub, redecorated two rooms, replaced window treatments, replaced the dishwasher, planted her favorite flowers, and did so much more. I used my hands to express love that she would not see unless and until she came home.

I exercised every day, walking an average of four miles a day, seven days a week.

I searched every word of the four Gospels for the example of how Christ loves and leads that I, as a husband, might love my wife as Christ loved the church and gave Himself for it. I chronicled my findings in a spreadsheet. (Upon re-reading it, I felt my work was doctrinally weak and will not be published.) However, for me, it was a good spiritual exercise.

I journaled.

I found ways to give financially.

I attended every church service and function and sought to do my part as a part of the family of God.

This list goes on and on. The point, though, is not to declare my goodness. The point is that an element of transformation starts and grows in the heart. Full commitment is not a method for achieving a goal; it is a fruit of repentance.

The Pharisees who haunted the LORD through His ministry on earth were separated, and they had good works. Nevertheless, those works did not impress John the Baptist. Are you caught in a vicious stronghold of sin? Have you considered John's rebuke?

But when he saw many of the Pharisees and Sadducees come to his baptism, he said unto them, O generation of vipers, who hath warned you to flee from the wrath to come? Bring forth therefore fruits meet for repentance: and think not to say within yourselves, We have Abraham to our father: for I say unto you, that God is able of these stones to raise up children unto Abraham. And now also the axe is laid unto the root of the trees: therefore every tree which bringeth not forth good fruit is hewn down, and cast into the fire. I indeed baptize you with water unto repentance. but he that cometh after me is mightier than I, whose shoes I am not worthy to bear: he shall baptize you with the Holy Ghost, and with fire: Whose fan is in his hand, and he will throughly purge his floor, and gather his wheat into the garner; but he will burn up the chaff with unquenchable fire (Matthew 3:7-12).

Are you caught in a vicious stronghold of sin? What shadow of intent is cast by the light of the good works men may see in your life so that they might glorify your father which is in Heaven? Do you hunger and thirst after righteousness? If so, is there any doubt that you will be filled? If not, is there any hope that you can be filled with HIS righteousness? What does repentance that causes the desire to seek and intermeddle with all wisdom look like? Does it look like the repentance David displayed in Psalm 51?

Have mercy upon me, O God, according to thy lovingkindness: according unto the multitude of thy tender mercies blot out my transgressions. Wash me thoroughly from mine iniquity, and cleanse me from my sin. For I acknowledge my transgressions: and my sin is ever before me.

Against thee, thee only, have I sinned, and done this evil in thy sight: that thou mightest be justified when thou speakest, and be clear when thou judgest. Behold, I was shapen in iniquity; and in sin did my mother conceive me. Behold, thou desirest truth in the inward parts: and in the hidden part thou shalt make me to know wisdom.

Purge me with hyssop, and I shall be clean: wash me, and I shall be whiter than snow. Make me to hear joy and gladness; that the bones which thou hast broken may rejoice. Hide thy face from my sins, and blot out all mine iniquities.

Create in me a clean heart, O God; and renew a right spirit within me. Cast me not away from thy presence; and take not thy holy spirit from me. Restore unto me the joy of thy salvation; and uphold me with thy free spirit. Then will I teach transgressors thy ways; and sinners shall be converted unto thee.

Deliver me from bloodguiltiness, O God, thou God of my salvation: and my tongue shall sing aloud of thy righteousness. O LORD, open thou my lips; and my mouth shall shew forth thy praise. For thou desirest not sacrifice; else would I give it: thou delightest not in burnt offering. The sacrifices of God are a broken spirit: a broken and a contrite heart, O God, thou wilt not despise.

*Do good in thy good pleasure unto Zion: build thou the walls of Jerusalem. Then shalt thou be pleased with the sacrifices of righteousness, with burnt offering and whole burnt offering: then shall they offer bullocks upon thine altar (*Psalm 51).

Surrender

To me, my surrender involved agreeing with God that His ways are better than my ways. I had sinned, and the consequences were in His hands. I submitted my heart to His hands and told Him that with or without Suzanne, I wanted His plan. With or without my appetites being filled, I wanted His timing. I am still working on this one, and sometimes I do better than other times.

It is my desire to want what God wants, but sometimes I do not. My surrender came through the night one Wednesday, but it has needed constant renewal. My root sin is pride, and the self-will that comes with it can still be a battle. I definitely had a real day of surrender, but I would be lying to myself to deny the continual struggle.

Embracing the Love of God

We love Him because He first loved us. He is love. The grace of a loving Heavenly Father sustains us—not the power of the supposedly omnipotent tyrant or bully who dominates some faiths.

Ephesians 2:1-7

And you hath he quickened, who were dead in trespasses and sins; wherein in time past ye walked according to the course of this world, according to the prince of the power of the air, the spirit that now worketh in the children of disobedience: among whom also we all had our conversation in times past in the lusts of our flesh, fulfilling the desires of the flesh and of the mind; and were by nature the children of wrath, even as others. But God, who is rich in mercy, for his great love wherewith he loved us, even when we were dead in sins, hath quickened us together with Christ, (by grace ye are saved;) and hath raised us up together, and made us sit together in heavenly places in Christ Jesus: that in the ages to come he might shew the exceeding riches of his grace in his kindness toward us through Christ Jesus...

Tearing Down Strongholds

For me, this was dealing with the sin of imaginations that exalt themselves against the knowledge of God. Having already covered this step in depth, I will forgo further or repetitious explanation here.

Building Vigilance

As of this writing, we still meet with a counselor monthly. I still speak with another on an impromptu basis. We continue reading. We have deferred some decisions until after we have been reunited even longer. We have been hurt; we do not want to be hurt again, and I do not want to do more damage. We cannot go back.

Helping Others

If God transforms one's life, does He do so only for the benefit of the one? *Freely ye have received; freely give.* Restoration to God is exhilarating, liberating, and spiritually thrilling. Sin is vanquished, and real results can be seen! Blessings flow like rivers carrying the redeemed in currents of grace! This is too good not to share!

God charges His children in Galatians 6, *Brethren, if a man be overtaken in a fault, ye which are spiritual, restore such an one in the spirit of meekness; considering thyself, lest thou also be tempted* (v. 1). The trouble with helping people is that they which are whole do not need physicians. Those who need physicians are sick, and sickness can spread.

He that walketh with wise men shall be wise: but a companion of fools shall be destroyed (Proverbs 13:20). In the depths of my pride, rage, and anger, I had plenty of foolishness in me. I knew the Biblical admonitions about people like me, such as Proverbs 22:24, which says, *Make no friendship with an angry man; and with a furious man thou shalt not go,* so what gives? People-a-plenty helped me! If we have received grace and help, should we not pass it on? Of course we should—but in the spirit of meekness, considering ourselves, because Satan WILL tempt us.

The enemy wants to steal, kill, and destroy. If he can draw the unprepared zealot to a drowning brother, both will go down. The first prerequisite for the helper is to be spiritual himself or herself. This does not mean merely the absence of the strongholds; it also means the presence of His grace in the helper's spirit. Helpers must walk with God and yield to the Holy Spirit.

Next, we need to be meek. We have to understand that we are not impervious to sin or its effects. Temptation is real, and spiritual darkness permeates this world. In helping others, we must walk with the caution that we would use in a physical rescue. Get your own footing firm before reaching to pull up another.

Let's be real. The fact that I have experienced victory does not make me an expert. Would you not agree? God warns us in James 3:1, *My brethren, be not many masters, knowing that we shall receive the greater condemnation.* Perhaps we have limits in whom we can help and how much we can offer? How would we know what those limits should be?

Jesus Himself said, *If I bear witness of myself, my witness is not true. There is another that beareth witness of me; and I know that the witness which he witnesseth of me is true* (John 5:31, 32). Would it be wise to trust another to tell you your limits?

Yes. Help others. That is why God helped you. Yes, make time; spend money, pray, cry, yearn, read, and seek. The rescued should become a rescuer, but do so in the spirit of meekness. Help like this:

Romans 12:3-8

For I say, through the grace given unto me, to every man that is among you, not to think of himself more highly than he ought to think; but to think soberly, according as God hath dealt to every man the measure of faith. For as we have many members in one body, and all members have not the same office: so we, being many, are one body in Christ, and every one members one of another. Having then gifts differing according to the grace that is given to us, whether prophecy, let us prophesy according to the proportion of faith; or ministry, let us wait on our ministering: or he that teacheth, on teaching; or he that exhorteth, on exhortation: he that giveth, let him do it with simplicity; he that ruleth, with diligence; he that sheweth mercy, with cheerfulness.

Let love be without dissimulation. Abhor that which is evil; cleave to that which is good. Be kindly affectioned one to another with brotherly love; in honour preferring one another; not slothful in business; fervent in spirit; serving the LORD; rejoicing in hope; patient in tribulation; continuing instant in prayer; distributing to the necessity of saints; given to hospitality. Bless them which persecute you: bless, and curse not. Rejoice with them that do rejoice, and weep with them that weep. Be of the same mind one toward another. Mind not high things, but condescend to men of low estate. Be not wise in your own conceits.

HOPEFUL HELPS

- Repent with your whole heart.
- Surrender to God's will and timing daily.
- Embrace the love of God.
- Tear down strongholds of imagination.
- Be vigilant.
- Beware of pride.

Thinking Ahead

If you and I were ever to play a game of catch, you would probably pick up on the unorthodox way I throw a baseball. My motion is halfway between normal and side-armed. I know the correct way to throw a ball, and I can model the motions fairly well, but when I attempt to toss a ball in that fashion, it is very unlikely to be catchable. My muscle memory wants my body to throw the ball in a certain way.

Our souls also seem to have muscle memory. We may refer to this as quirks, personality, or peculiarities, but we all have habitual ways of performing tasks. For thirty years my way of dealing with many of life's issues was to respond in pride and to dominate. Satan is aware of such weaknesses, and as a child of God, you can trust the kingdom of darkness to attack you in those areas.

Before Suzanne came home, I lost more than fifty-five pounds. I was living a rather disciplined life, which included daily exercise and disciplined eating. As I write this, I have put back on no less than twenty of those pounds.

When we experience spiritual victory, the Deceiver's plan for our lives is for us to slip back into our old sins. I grieve to think of our friends from Reformers Unanimous who have gained victory over addiction, only to be taken captive again by Satan. If in political arenas, the price of freedom is eternal vigilance, then certainly in spiritual arenas, the price of holy living is to be *stedfast, unmoveable, always abounding in the work of the LORD.* (I Corinthians 15:58)

Jesus taught the same parable to teach two different lessons, and His words seem apropos here:

When the unclean spirit is gone out of a man, he walketh through dry places, seeking rest, and findeth none. Then he saith, I will return into my house from whence I came out; and when he is come, he findeth it empty, swept, and garnished. Then goeth he, and taketh with himself seven other spirits more wicked than himself, and they enter in and dwell there: and the last state of that man is worse than the first (Matthew 12:43-45).

The man in this parable consciously decided to return to the place he knew—the place of his comfort. Beware; that which is begun in faith cannot be completed in the flesh. In Galatians 3:1-6, Paul warns the church of this matter:

O foolish Galatians, who hath bewitched you, that ye should not obey the truth, before whose eyes Jesus Christ hath been evidently set forth, crucified among you? This only would I learn of you, Received ye the Spirit by the works of the law, or by the hearing of faith? Are ye so foolish? having begun in the Spirit, are ye now made perfect by the flesh? Have ye suffered so many things in vain? if it be yet in vain. He therefore that ministereth to you the Spirit, and worketh miracles among you, doeth he it by the works of the law, or by the hearing of faith? Even as Abraham believed God, and it was accounted to him for righteousness.

Let it not be so said of us, my brethren. If we have known the way of peace, let us keep the way of peace. Let us keep our hearts with all diligence, for out of them are the issues of life.

Redemption does not make a person spiritual, but redemption does seal the child of God with the spirit of promise. To those of us who have received Him, He gave the *power to become the sons of God, even to us who believe on His name* (John 1:12). That power, that redemptive power that outshines a million suns, is realized by the same faith that brings salvation. Sanctification is God's work of setting His child apart to Himself as he submits to Him in faith. Though nothing is good in my flesh, there is nothing but good in His Spirit. He is ready to deliver us from any work of the flesh to every fruit of the Spirit, but He must do His work. In very truth, we who begin in faith MUST be made perfect in faith.

In James 1:19-25, the LORD's half-brother, James, instructs the angry along these very lines:

Wherefore, my beloved brethren, let every man be swift to hear, slow to speak, slow to wrath: for the wrath of man worketh not the righteousness of God. Wherefore lay apart all filthiness and superfluity of naughtiness, and receive with meekness the engrafted word, which is able to save your souls.

But be ye doers of the word, and not hearers only, deceiving your own selves. For if any be a hearer of the word, and not a doer, he is like unto a man beholding his natural face in a glass: for he beholdeth himself, and goeth his way, and straightway forgetteth what manner of man he was. But whoso looketh into the perfect law of liberty, and continueth therein, he being not a forgetful hearer, but a doer of the work, this man shall be blessed in his deed.

Strong's Concordance defines the naughtiness of Verse 21 in this way:
1.   malignity, malice, ill-will, desire to injure
2.   wickedness, depravity
     a. wickedness that is not ashamed to break laws
3.   evil, trouble

The soul of God's child is made free when he receives with meekness the engrafted word. As a sprig from one tree is grafted into another, becoming one tree, or as engrafted skin takes root and grows where it is placed, so must the Word of God become a living part of the Christian's soul. As God's children we can know the truth about ourselves by simply looking into the mirror of God's Word, but too often, we go our way, forgetting what we have seen.

Have you ever listened to a Bible lesson or sermon, agreed with it, or even found inspiration in it, only to be unable to recall it a few days later? When we do so, we fail to receive the Word with faith, meekness, or diligence. To be a doer of the Word, we must meditate therein. As the LORD told Joshua,

This book of the law shall not depart out of thy mouth; but thou shalt meditate therein day and night, that thou mayest observe to do according to all that is written therein: for then thou shalt make thy way prosperous, and then thou shalt have good success (Joshua 1:8).

Good success is my prayer for every brother or sister recovering from the snare of the Devil. As you make your journey from flesh to faith, *Study to shew thyself approved unto God, a workman that needeth not to be ashamed, rightly dividing the word of truth* (II Timothy 2:15). Be a doer of the Word, and not a hearer only.

Perhaps Mr. Longfellow had such ideas in mind:

A Psalm of Life
BY HENRY WADSWORTH LONGFELLOW
Tell me not, in mournful numbers,
Life is but an empty dream!
For the soul is dead that slumbers,
And things are not what they seem.
Life is real! Life is earnest!
And the grave is not its goal;
Dust thou art, to dust returnest,
Was not spoken of the soul.

Not enjoyment, and not sorrow,
Is our destined end or way;
But to act, that each to-morrow
Find us farther than to-day.
Art is long, and Time is fleeting,
And our hearts, though stout and brave,
Still, like muffled drums, are beating
Funeral marches to the grave.
In the world's broad field of battle,
In the bivouac of Life,
Be not like dumb, driven cattle!
Be a hero in the strife!
Trust no Future, howe'er pleasant!
Let the dead Past bury its dead!
Act,— act in the living Present!
Heart within, and God o'erhead!
Lives of great men all remind us
We can make our lives sublime,
And, departing, leave behind us
Footprints on the sands of time;
Footprints, that perhaps another,
Sailing o'er life's solemn main,
A forlorn and shipwrecked brother,
Seeing, shall take heart again.
Let us, then, be up and doing,
With a heart for any fate;
Still achieving, still pursuing,
Learn to labor and to wait.

HOPEFUL HELPS

- Be eternally vigilant.
- Beware of pride.

Facing Facts

In October of 2003, right in the middle of the years of improvement, I took my son to Florida for a few days. The gals at our church were having a ladies' conference, and our house was going to be overstuffed with females. For we males, the time was ripe to "get out of Dodge."

My son has always been quite athletic, and I, his chubby father with a touch of asthma, cannot claim that same distinction. On Friday we had complimentary hopper passes to Disney, but what were we to do with Thursday? Being a geek, I have long believed that all answers are on the Internet. If you were to tell me that the answers are in the Bible, I would calmly remind you that the Bible IS on the Internet, so there I searched. I found the answer: ocean-going Jet Skis™!

The guy who rented us the Jet Ski™ was on the Atlantic Coast of Florida, but he had the accent of a valley girl. "Dude! Speed is your friend! If you slow these suckers down too fast, the nose will dip into the waves. Dude! If that happens, just let go! Just let go, and you'll like totally flip into the water, but it's totally, like cool. It's easy to get up on one of these bad boys, but if you hang on, you will totally turn it over. Dude, it is radically difficult to right a Jet Ski™ in the ocean by yourself. JUST LET GO! Like dude! What a day! You are totally the only ocean-going craft in twenty-five square miles of ocean! Have a blast, and speed is your friend!" With that speech, we were off. After puttering slowly past the point that indicated we were safely out of the way of manatees, we took off! Of course, we operated with the throttle completely wide open the whole time.

At first we were speeding straight across the tops of the two-to-three foot waves as fast as we could go, but that quickly became boring. My son was at my back, and I found that if I did s-curves at full throttle, I could soak him without getting terribly wet myself. That did not become boring, but it did get a bit scary, and as predicted, I slowed down too quickly, dipping the nose of the Jet Ski into the waves. I let go.

I landed just a few feet to the starboard side of the Jet Ski™. The emergency shutoff tethered around my wrist killed the engine, and the Jet Ski™ stopped, waiting patiently for me to return with the key from my wrist so that we could continue on our adventure. My son was still seated calmly, though helplessly, on the back.

Being a horrible swimmer, I put my head down and started swimming with all I had to close the few feet between my son and me. Shortly, I lifted my head and found myself twenty yards farther from my son than when I had started swimming. Splash! A wave came from behind me and washed entirely over my head. "Valley Boy" was wrong; this was NOT totally cool!

I had never before heard of rip currents, and I am a terrible swimmer. I tried shouting instructions to my stranded son, but my attempts were in vain. I had to turn my back on him to face the oncoming waves so that I could ride them and not be washed over by each one.

The emergency shut-off was around my wrist. The car keys were around my neck. My son was a long way from shore and perhaps two miles from the put-in point. He was also an hour's drive from the hotel and a thousand miles from home. The cell phones were locked in the trunk. "Only ocean-going craft in twenty-five square miles of ocean" rang in my ears. The statement was no lie. My son was alone.

Just minutes before my riptide swept form seemed destined to be carried under the northern bridge and into the open Atlantic, I spotted a speedboat. It was far enough away that I could barely make out that it was one man alone, flying open-throttle toward my son. I turned toward him and began shouting. A wave immediately washed over me, but I did not care. I kept shouting, and presently the boat slowed, then stopped. The driver did not look my way but searched his boat.

After a couple more waves sent saltwater into my open mouth, he stood on the bow of his boat and looked my way. Then he came toward me. Looking into the water, he asked, "What are you doing here?" I was an incredibly long way from any place that made sense, but I quickly explained. He knew where the Jet Ski™ rental was. He welcomed me into his boat and took me in that direction. Once my son came into view, we headed straight toward him, and the driver saw me safely back onto the Jet Ski™ with my son. He waited until he heard the engine roar to life and then sped away himself. I never learned his name. For some strange reason, friends and family will not go on Jet Skis™ with me.

Back to the main story.

Suzanne and I had been back together less than eight months the first time we celebrated her birthday together. Before she left, I had planned a romantic getaway in Brown County, Indiana, a beautiful springtime destination. Less than a week after she left, I contacted the owner of the Airbnb where we had planned to stay with a notice along the lines of, "I need to cancel our romantic getaway. My wife left me." Because of that, for this first birthday after reconciliation, I booked us in a gorgeous Airbnb in Brown County.

On Suzanne's birthday, I casually mentioned that this date a year earlier had been very hard for me. I had seen pictures of her on Facebook with huge smiles, having a wonderful time just days after leaving me. In the course of the conversation, I told her that my selfish heart had wanted her to be grieved that she was without me on such a day. In a voice with more kindness than can be imagined by any but her closest friends, she set the record straight:

"I was running from you."

That Suzanne said that was important for more than one reason. First, her freedom in making that statement established the fact that eight months into our new marriage, she was free to speak the truth with no fear of retaliation. Anger did not enter my soul for a nanosecond. It also reminded me that I did not have nearly thirty-one years of wedded bliss. I had eight months of a very good marriage with thirty years of baggage. Mine was still the face of the abuser, and so shall it ever be. I have sown to the flesh, and of the flesh I have reaped corruption.

Books about how to reconcile after abuse are very rare. In fact, I do not know of one. Counselors who recommend reconciliation after abuse are hard to find. Who can take such a position? Could anyone casually recommend a friend to go back into a burning building to retrieve even the most valuable and treasured of possessions? If not, how much more absurd would it be to ask a girl to go back to an abusive man? If she goes back and dies at his hands or if she goes back and suffers more, what of the advice to go back?

To get on a Jet Ski™ with me is much less threatening than it is to send a beloved daughter, sister, mother, or friend back into the fires of a hellish marriage. Because of their love for Suzanne, precious few people were for her return, especially in our particular timing. Precious few people will be for any reconciliation after abuse. Transformation is hard to confirm; people are more volatile than the ocean, and results cannot be guaranteed.

There is hope, but there are no promises outside of Providence. Have you been abusive? You can in very deed be redeemed by the Prince of Peace. You can be different in time and eternity. You can live a peaceful, godly life full of reward and grace, but you cannot know that reconciliation is an option until she believes that it is so. You can only be reconciled to a godly marriage by the mercy of God.

Have you been abused? You can heal, and you can have a godly, rewarding life. You cannot guarantee (nor can he) that the abuser will be redeemed. Only the miraculous hand of a loving God can bring a person to that point.

In every case of separation, I want reconciliation. I believe that Christ stated clearly that He and the Father are never, ever for divorce. Only for the hardness of our hearts and in cases of fornication or abandonment does God permit making such a choice.

When a man leaves his house in handcuffs after hurting his spouse, has he abandoned her in unbelief? What if the authorities never come, but could have? If a precious daughter of the King must flee for safety and if the object of her fear cannot be proven safe, who has abandoned whom? I cannot answer these questions. Expecting a counselor or an abused spouse to answer them in your particular way is patently unfair.

By all means, if you have suffered, perpetrated, or encountered abuse, go forward in grace. Go forward in love. Go forward in caution. Go forward in prayer. Go forward, *forgetting those things which are behind, and reaching forth unto those things which are before;* (**and**) *press for the mark of the high calling of God in Christ Jesus* (Philippians 3:13-14).

I do not pretend to be an expert or an authority. I am the redeemed former monster of a true-to-life horror story. I have never published a book before, and I can only hope that this one has been helpful.

I am simply your humble servant, acknowledging who and what I am, and praying that the *God of all comfort who comforteth us in all our tribulation* (**may enable me to comfort you**) *with the same comfort wherewith* (**I myself**) *have been comforted of God* (II Corinthians 1:3, 4).

Thank you for reading.

Connecting

We want to hear from you! This book was written to be a help to victims and perpetrators of domestic abuse and to provide encouragement to pastors, ministry leaders, and advocates. We want to provide help, encouragement, and resources where we can.

We are continuing to educate ourselves about the problem of domestic abuse and about the solutions also. Our journey has only begun, and we look forward to what God has for us in the future.

If you have a question, a comment, a testimony or a suggestion, please contact us directly by emailing info@redemptivehope.com.

If this text has been helpful to you, please leave a review with your favorite book seller so that others will know.

At the time of this writing, www.redemptivehope.com is in development. Please check in from time to time to see our progress.

Recommended Reading List

- *A Biblical Perspective of What to Do When You Are Abused by Your Husband*, Debi Pryde
- *A Faith Full Marriage: Building a Lifetime Love on Biblical Principles*, Paul Chappell
- *A Shepherd Looks at Psalm 23*, W. Phillip Keller
- *Choosing Forgiveness; Your Journey to Freedom,* Nancy Leigh DeMoss
- *Crazy Love*, Francis Chan
- *Debilitated and Diminished: Help for Christian Women in Emotionally Abusive Marriages*, Dr. Anne Dryburgh
- *Emotionally Healthy Spirituality*, Peter Scazzero
- *Forgiveness*, Harold Vaughan
- *How to Help People Change,* Jay E. Adams
- *Love and Respect*, Dr. Emerson Eggerichs
- *Replace Anger: A Radically Refreshing Approach*, Anonymous (ISBN-10: 9780692297926)
- *The Case of the "Hopeless" Marriage*, Jay E. Adams
- *The Emotionally Destructive Marriage*, Leslie Vernick
- *The Exemplary Husband*, Stuart Scott
- *The Heart of Domestic Abuse*, Chris Moles
- *The Slight Edge*, Jeff Olson
- *They Meant it for Evil*, Lucinda Pennington
- *Why Am I So Angry*, Debi Pryde

Resources

Association of Certified Biblical Counselors, ACBC, serves counselors by providing contact information for training and conferences. The *Find A Counselor* page allows one to find a counselor by need and location.
https://biblicalcounseling.com/
https://biblicalcounseling.com/counselors/

The Biblical Counseling Coalition provides opportunities for Christian Counselors to connect and to share resources. It provides articles, podcasts and other resources for counselors.
http://biblicalcounselingcoalition.org

Called to Peace Ministries
https://www.calledtopeace.org
https://vimeo.com/user24998836/videos
https://joyforrest.wordpress.com
A ministry "dedicated to offering hope and healing to victims of domestic violence, emotionally destructive relationships, and sexual assault." The Vimeo page has helpful videos. The WordPress page is the home to Joy's blog.

Caring for the Heart Ministries provides excellent counseling, training, and helpful written materials. The website also lists counselors trained for the program. Caring for the Heart is supported by donations. Counseling is generally free to counselees.
https://caringfortheheart.com

Chris Moles is the Senior Pastor of Grace Community Chapel; a Certified Biblical Counselor, facilitator, a coach for abusive men seeking redemption, and an author.
http://www.chrismoles.org/
https://www.youtube.com/channel/UCKGtQcZMzX-x6Jmr2-n_S3Q/

Debi Pryde is a biblical counselor for ladies, a speaker, and an author.
http://www.debipryde.com/

The Domestic Abuse Intervention Programs (DAIP) was one of the first organizations to address domestic abuse. Their model for understanding abuse is the standard many counselors use. They provide training for counselors and organizations that hope to help perpetrators become peaceful.
https://www.theduluthmodel.org/

Focus Ministries:
https://www.focusministries1.org/
Focus Ministries has free and paid resources. It sponsors support groups and provides training.

The Institute for Biblical Counseling & Discipleship provides articles, handouts, and recorded lessons on the topic of abuse.
https://ibcd.org/topics/abuse

National Domestic Violence Hotline:
1-800-799-7233; 1-800-787-3224 (TTY);
https://www.thehotline.org/
https://www.ourchildinfo.com provides a resource for those who still need to communicate with a spouse who shares kids.

Psalm 82 Initiative
https://www.patreon.com/Psalm82
The Psalm 82 Initiative exists to help churches and their leaders recognize and respond to abuse in the church more effectively.

Revive Our Hearts
https://www.reviveourhearts.com
ROH provides a radio program, podcasts, conferences, and many helpful materials. ROH describes itself as "Calling Women to Freedom, Fullness, and Fruitfulness in Christ."

To the best of our ability, and for the foreseeable future, we will endeavor to keep this list updated on our website.

References

Adams, J. (2007) *The Case of the Hopeless Marriage: A Nouthetic Counseling Case from Beginning to End.* Stanley, NC: Timeless Texts.

Currington, S. B. (2010). *Recovery Through God's Truth: 10 Principles of Freedom for the Addicted Nation.* Rockford, IL: Wesscott Marketing Inc.

Meyer, J. (2015). Fooled By False Leadership. Minneapolis: Bethlehem Baptist Church.

Scazzero, P. (2107). *Emotionally Healthy Spirituality: It's Impossible to Be Spiritually Mature, While Remaining Emotionally Immature.* New York: Zondervan.

www.ingramcontent.com/pod-product-compliance
Lightning Source LLC
Chambersburg PA
CBHW060336030426
42336CB00011B/1364